History 4
Learning Coach Guide

Part 1

About K12 Inc.

K12 Inc., a technology-based education company, is the nation's leading provider of proprietary curriculum and online education programs to students in grades K–12. K12 provides its curriculum and academic services to online schools, traditional classrooms, blended school programs, and directly to families. K12 Inc. also operates the K12 International Academy, an accredited, diploma-granting online private school serving students worldwide. K12's mission is to provide any child the curriculum and tools to maximize success in life, regardless of geographic, financial, or demographic circumstances. K12 Inc. is accredited by CITA. More information can be found at www.K12.com.

Printed by R.R. Donnelley, Kendallville, IN, USA, May 2016

Table of Contents

Learning Coach Guide
Lesson 1. Optional: Maps and Globes: Directions and Hemispheres

Globes, maps, and satellite images are important tools that help us understand the Earth.

Lesson Objectives

- Identify the seven continents and four oceans.
- Use cardinal and intermediate directions to interpret information on maps.
- Use map keys to interpret information on maps.
- Analyze political maps to gain information.
- Distinguish between absolute and relative location.
- Use lines of latitude and longitude to identify location.
- Use map scale to calculate distances between places,
- Identify different kinds of information provided by a globe, a map, and a satellite image.
- Locate specified places relative to the Equator, prime meridian or Earth's hemispheres.
- Demonstrate mastery of important geographic knowledge and skills.

PREPARE

Approximate lesson time is 60 minutes.

Materials

> For the Adult
> > 📖 Lesson Answer Key

Lesson Notes

For students who have taken previous grades in K12's History program, most of the material in today's lesson is a review. Students might want to read the workbook material and answer some of the questions to reinforce their prior knowledge. They should take the assessment. Students new to K12 who have not studied the material presented in this lesson should read the workbook carefully and answer all questions. These students might want to extend this lesson over two (or more) days, perhaps focusing on one workbook activity per day.

For a valuable additional resource, visit the National Geographic education website on maps and geography. Find information and teaching tools, learn about the National Geography Standards, and check out some online adventures.

Keywords and Pronunciation

cardinal directions : The four main directions (north, south, east, and west).

compass rose : A symbol showing the directions on a map.

continent : One of the seven large areas of land on Earth.

Equator : An imaginary line around the middle of the Earth, halfway between the North and the South Poles.

hemisphere : One half of the Earth; the Earth can be divided into four hemispheres (Eastern, Western, Northern, and Southern).

intermediate directions : The directions in between the cardinal directions (northwest, northeast, southwest, and southeast).

---

map key : A guide to what the symobls on a map mean.

physical map : A map showing the Earth's natural features, such as rivers, lakes, and mountains.

prime meridian (priym muh-RIH-dee-uhn) : An imaginary line going around the Earth and running through the North and South Poles.

relative location : The location of one place in relation to another place.

satellite image : A picture of the Earth taken from space.

TEACH

Activity 1. Optional: Optional Lesson Instructions (Online)

Notes

This lesson is OPTIONAL. It is provided for students who seek enrichment or extra practice. You may skip this lesson.

If you choose to skip this lesson, then go to the Plan or Lesson Lists page and mark this lesson "Skipped" in order to proceed to the next lesson in the course.

Activity 2. Optional: Maps and Globes (Online)

Instructions

- Read and discuss Activity 1 "Maps and Globes" on pages 4–9 of Understanding Geography.
- Have your student answer Questions 1–21 in his History Journal.
- If he has time, he may want to answer Questions 22-26 and the Skill Builder Questions on page 9. They are optional.
- After he has finished the workbook activity, he should come back online to play the Oceans and Continents game.

Activity 3. Optional: Hemispheres and Directions (Online)

ASSESS

Optional. Wrap-Up: Maps and Globes: Directions and Hemispheres (Online)

Students will complete an offline assessment based on the lesson objectives. Print the assessment and have students complete it on their own. Use the answer key to score the assessment, and then enter the results online. The attached answer key is the most current and may not coincide with previously printed guides.

Maps and Globes: Directions and Hemispheres Answer Key

Activity 1: Maps and Globes

1. See the map on page 4.
2. See the map on page 4.
3. The continents you can see are Europe, Africa, Asia, Australia, and Antarctica. You can see the Indian Ocean. (You can also see parts of the Pacific, Atlantic, and Arctic Oceans, but they are not labeled.)
4. North America = 1
   South America = 2
   Europe = 4
   Asia = 5
   Africa = 3
   Antarctica = 7
   Australia = 6
5. Atlantic Ocean = c
   Pacific Ocean = b
   Indian Ocean = d
   Arctic Ocean = a
6. The rivers in Asia include the Indus, Ganges, Ob, Yenisey, Lena, Amur, Yellow, Yangtze, and Mekong. (You only need to name two.)
7. The mountain ranges in Asia are the Caucasus Mountains, Zagros Mountains, Ural Mountains, Verkhoyansk Range, Altay Mountains, Tian Shan, Kunlun Mountains, and the Himalaya. (You only need to name three.)
8. Mount Everest is the highest point. It is 29,035 feet high.
9. The lowest point is the Dead Sea. It is 1,365 feet below sea level.
10. The Indian Ocean, Pacific Ocean, and Arctic Ocean border on Asia.
11. You can see Europe, Africa, and Australia.
12. The Ural Mountains and the Caucasus Mountains separate Europe from Asia.
13. Tokyo is the capital.
14. Mount Fuji is near Tokyo.
15. Other cities on the map include Sapporo, Nagano, Nagoya, Kyoto, Osaka, Hiroshima, Fukuoka, and Nagasaki (You only need to name two.)
16. Yes, there is an airport near Saporo.
17. Yes, there is a temple near Kyoto.
18. Sea of Japan
19. The gardens in Tokyo include Shinjuku-Gyoen Garden, Meiji Jingu Outer Gardens, and the Hamarikyu Garden.
20. Harajuku Station is close to Yoyogi Park.
21. The two shrines are the Meiji Jingu Shrine and the Yasukuni Shrine.

Optional
22. Tokyo Expressway No. 4
23. You could visit the Meiji Jingu Outer Gardens or the Shinjuku-Gyoen Garden. (You only need to name one.)
24. The shrine is in Yoyogi Park.
25. National Theater
26. Nezu Art Museum

Skill Builder
1. globe
2. satellite image
3. The continents are North America, South America, Europe, Africa, Asia, Australia, and Antarctica. The oceans are the Atlantic, Pacific, Indian, and Arctic Oceans.
4. Arctic Ocean
5. Atlantic Ocean, Arctic Ocean
6. Africa, Asia, Australia, and Antarctica touch the Indian Ocean. (You only need to name two.)
7. Aconcagua is the highest point in South America.
8. Lake Eyre is the lowest point in Australia.
9. The Nile and the Congo are two important rivers in Africa.
10. The Rocky Mountains and Appalachian Mountains are in North America.
11. The Andes are in South America.
12. The Alps are in Europe.

Activity 2: Directions and Hemispheres

1. Western Hemisphere
2. Eastern Hemisphere
3. Northern Hemisphere
4. North America is located in the Northern and Western Hemispheres.
5. Australia is located in the Southern and Eastern Hemispheres.
6. The Equator crosses South America, Africa, and Asia and the Pacific, Atlantic, and Indian Oceans.
7. The prime meridian crosses Europe, Africa, and Antarctica and the Arctic and Atlantic Oceans.
8. North is at the top of map.
9. Pyramid of Menkaure
10. You would walk west from the Sphinx to the pyramid of Khafre.

Optional
11. You would walk southwest from the pyramid of Khufu.
12. From the ticket booth you would head south to the pyramid of Khufu, then west and south to the pyramid of Khafre, and finally farther south to the pyramid of Menkaure.
13. Niger is directly north of Nigeria. Other countries farther north of Nigeria are Algeria, Libya, and Tunisia. (You only need to name two.)

14. Libya
15. Answers may vary. If you headed southeast from Angola, you would cross part of Namibia to reach Botswana and South Africa. Zambia, Zimbabwe, Swaziland, Lesotho, and Mozambique could also be considered southeast of Angola. (You only need to name two.)
16. southeast
17. west
18. north

Skill Builder
1. Northern and Southern
2. Eastern and Western
3. Northern and Eastern
4. Asia
5. South America
6. The shortest route to North America would be to travel northeast.
7. You would travel southeast to reach the Indian Ocean.
8. South is behind, west is to the left, and east is to the right.
9. relative

Lesson Assessment Answer Key

Maps and Globes: Directions and Hemispheres

Answers:

1. globe

2. Using the criteria listed below, enter the number of points your student earned based on the number of correctly labeled items.

Did your student identify and label 10 - 11 items correctly?	50 points
Did your student identify and label 7 - 9 items correctly?	40 points
Did your student identify and label 4 - 6 items correctly?	25 points
Did your student identify and label 2 - 3 items correctly?	10 points
Did your student identify and label 1 item correctly?	5 points
Was your student unable to identify and label a single item correctly?	0 points

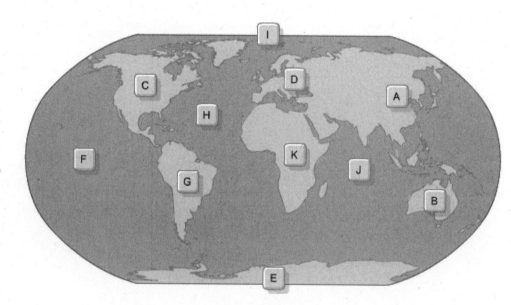

A. Asia

B. Australia

C. North America

D. Europe

E. Antarctica

F. Pacific Ocean

G. South America

H. Atlantic Ocean

I. Arctic Ocean

J. Indian Ocean

K. Africa

3. Europe
4. Shimbash Station
5. southwest
6. Southern and Eastern Hemispheres

Learning Coach Guide
Lesson 2: Political Maps and Map Scales

On political maps, colors and symbols guide you as you search for countries, states, and cities. But how big are they? How far apart are they? Scales will give you those answers.

Lesson Objectives

- Explore concepts to be addressed during the year in History 4.
- Identify political maps as those showing the borders of countries or states.
- Distinguish between countries and continents.
- Analyze political maps to gain information.
- Use a map scale to calculate distances between places.
- Distinguish between large-scale and small-scale maps.

PREPARE

Approximate lesson time is 60 minutes.

Advance Preparation

- It's important that you read the Course Introduction for History 4 before your student begins the course. You can find the course introduction at the beginning of the Political Maps and Map Scales lesson.

Materials

For the Student

Understanding Geography: Map Skills and Our World (Level 4)

History Journal

For the Adult

🖳 Lesson Answer Key

Lesson Notes

For students who have taken previous grades in K12's History program, most of the material in today's lesson is a review. Students might want to read the workbook material and answer some of the questions to reinforce their prior knowledge. They should take the assessment. Students new to K12 who have not studied the material presented in this lesson should read the workbook carefully and answer all questions. These students might want to extend this lesson over two (or more) days, perhaps focusing on one workbook activity per day.

TEACH
Activity 1: Welcome to History 4 *(Online)*
Instructions
Your student will navigate through a Course Introduction to learn about the organization and lesson layout of K12 History 4. The interactive Course Introduction will explain the different kinds of lessons offered—from online explorations to offline activities like map work and stories, to lesson assessments. Join your student in navigating the Course Introduction for an orientation of this year's History course.

Activity 2: Continents, Countries, and Capitals *(Online)*
Instructions
- Read and discuss Activity 3, "Continents, Countries, and Capitals," on pages 16–19 of *Understanding Geography*.
- Your student should answer Questions 1–18 in his History Journal.
- If he has time, he may want to answer the Skill Builder Questions on page 19. They are optional.

Activity 3: Distances *(Online)*

Activity 4. Optional: Political Maps and Map Scale *(Online)*
Instructions
In this optional online activity, your student can visit a website with an atlas of the United States. It features satellite-image color relief maps of each state.

ASSESS
Lesson Assessment: Political Maps and Map Scales (*Online*)
Students will complete an online assessment based on the lesson objectives. The assessment will be scored by the computer. The attached answer key is the most current and may not coincide with previously printed guides.

Political Maps and Map Scales Answer Key

Activity 3: Continents, Countries, and Capitals

1. The capital cities of the following countries are:
   Canada = Ottawa
   United States = Washington, D.C.
   Mexico = Mexico City
   Honduras = Tegucigalpa,
   Haiti = Port-au-Prince
2. eastern
3. Costa Rica and Panama
4. You would fly to the northeast.
5. You would travel southeast.
6. Guatemala
7. The following capitals are east of Havana, Cuba : Kingston, Jamaica ; Nassau, Bahamas; Port-au-Prince, Haiti; Santo Domingo, Dominican Republic; Port of Spain, Trinidad and Tobago. (You only need to name two.)
8. Canada and the United States, (Guatemala, Honduras, Nicaragua, Costa Rica, and Panama also touch both oceans because the Caribbean Sea is an arm of the Atlantic Ocean. You only need to name two.)
9. Panama, Costa Rica, Nicaragua, Honduras, Guatemala (You only need to name two.)
10. Mississippi
11. Chattahoochee River
12. Louisiana, Mississippi, Tennessee, Arkansas, and Missouri border the Mississippi. (The river also borders Illinois, which is not labeled on the map.)
13. Baton Rouge = Louisiana
    Tallahassee = Florida
    Raleigh = North Carolina
14. Baton Rouge, Lousiana; Jackson, Mississippi; Little Rock, Arkansas, and Nashville, Tennessee are west of Montgomery. (You only need to name two.)
15. Baton Rouge, Louisiana; Jackson, Mississippi; Little Rock, Arkansas; Tallahassee, Florida; Montgomery, Alabama; Atlanta, Georgia; and Columbia, South Carolina, are south of Nashville. (You only need to name two.)
16. You would travel southwest.
17. Virginia, North Carolina, South Carolina, Georgia, and Florida border on the Atlantic.
18. Florida, Alabama, Mississippi, Louisiana, and Texas border on the Gulf of Mexico.

Skill Builder
1. Political maps show the locations of countries and the borders between them, states, and cities.
2. Great Lakes
3. Río Grande
4. star

5. Boise = Idaho
   Phoenix = Arizona
   Jackson = Mississippi
   Harrisburg = Pennsylvania
   Augusta = Maine
6. Colorado River
7. New York, Canada, Michigan, Wisconsin
8. Argentina = South America
   China = Asia
   France = Europe
   Chad = Africa,
   Peru = South America

Activity 4: Distances

1. About 750 miles or 1,200 km
2. About 2,250 miles or 3,600 km
3. About 1,500 miles or 2,400 km
4. 1 mile
5. 2 ½ miles
6. 3 kilometers
7. 4 miles (2 miles each way)
8. 4 miles, about 5 ½ miles

<u>Skill Builder</u>
1. The city map of Portland, Oregon, has the largest scale. The map of the United States has the smallest scale.
2. The distance from New York City to Los Angeles is about 2,400 miles (3,800 kilometers). The distance from Detroit to Miami is about 1,200 miles (1,900 kilometers). The distance from Houston to Denver is about 800 miles (1,300 kilometers).

Learning Coach Guide
Lesson 3: Grids Show the Way

By learning to understand the coordinate system, students will be able to use latitude and longitude data to locate any place on Earth. Students will also learn to distinguish between absolute and relative location.

Lesson Objectives

- Express or identify a location using longitude and latitude.
- Identify lines of longitude and how they help determine location.
- Distinguish between absolute and relative location.
- Recognize that lines of latitude are also called parallels, and lines of longitude are also called meridians.
- Identify lines of latitude and how they help determine location.

PREPARE

Approximate lesson time is 60 minutes.

Materials

For the Student

Understanding Geography: Map Skills and Our World (Level 4)

History Journal

For the Adult

💻 Lesson Answer Key

Keywords and Pronunciation

degree : A unit of measure used to tell how far north or south of the Equator and east or west of the prime meridian a place is located.

latitude (LA-tuh-tood) : Parallel lines that run east and west on a map or globe and measure distance north and south.

longitude (LAHN-juh-tood) : Lines that run from the North Pole to the South Pole on a map or globe and measure distance east and west.

prime meridian (priym muh-RIH-dee-uhn) : An imaginary line that runs between the North and South Poles and divides the Earth into the Eastern and Western Hemispheres.

relative location : The location of one place in relation to another place.

TEACH
Activity 1: Grids Show the Way (Offline)

Activity 2: Grids Show the Way *(Offline)*

Instructions

In this optional offline activity, the student will make a list of cities that are identified only by their longitude and latitude coordinates, and then challenge other people to identify the cites.

ASSESS

Lesson Assessment: Grids Show the Way (*Online*)

Students will complete an online assessment based on the lesson objectives. The assessment will be scored by the computer. The attached answer key is the most current and may not coincide with previously printed guides.

Grids Show the Way Answer Key

Activity 5: The Coordinate System

1. Answers may vary. Accept any answer between 10° N and 15° N.
2. Answers may vary. Accept any answer between 30° S and 40° S.
3. Answers may vary. Accept any answer between 30° N and 35° N.
4. Answers may vary. Accept any answer between 30° S and 40° S.
5. Berlin
6. Cape Town
7. New York City is around 40° N.
8. Spain extends almost to 44° N.
9. Madrid is located slightly north of 40° N.
10. The strait is located at 36° N.
11. Africa extends slightly west of 15° W and east to approximately 50° E.
12. Los Angeles is near 120° W.
13. Beijing is near 120° E.
14. New Orleans
15. Vienna
16. South Africa extends westward to almost to 16° E; it extends eastward to slightly beyond 33° E.
17. The longitude of Cape Town is between 18° and 19° E.
18. The longitude of Johannesburg is about 28° E.
19. The longitude of Durban is about 31° E.
20. Lesotho extends about 2° (27° E to 29° E).
21. Pretoria and East London
22. New Orleans is about 30° N, 90° W.
23. Cairo is about 30° N, 30° E.
24. Shanghai is about 30° N, 120° E.
25. London and Accra are along the prime meridian.
26. New Orleans, Cairo, New Delhi, Shanghai are near 30° N. Vancouver and London are close to 50° N. (You only have to name two.)
27. Asia
28. South America
29. Australia
30. North America
31. Equator
32. Dayton
33. Canton

Optional

34. 41° N, 82° W
35. 40° N, 83° W
36. Ohio extends north to about 42° N and south to almost 38° N.
37. Ohio extends east to about 81° W and west to almost 85° W.

Skill Builder

1. New Orleans
2. Minneapolis or St. Paul, MN
3. Montana, Wyoming, Utah, Arizona
4. 40° N, 75° W
5. 40° N, 105° W
6. Northern Hemisphere, Western Hemisphere. You can tell by looking at the degrees of latitude and longitude.
7. latitude
8. Parallel is another word for a line of latitude.
9. coordinate system

Try It Yourself

- Russia
- Australia
- Mexico

Learning Coach Guide
Lesson 1: What's So Modern About the Modern World?

This lesson reviews history before the 1600s and introduces the modern world. The amazing discoveries of the Scientific Revolution led the way to the world we live in today. Thinking about the remarkable contrasts of the past and present sets the stage for understanding and exploring the period of history that began in the 1600s.

Lesson Objectives

- Describe the Scientific Revolution as a time of great progress in understanding nature.
- Explain that scientists used new methods of experimentation, obversation, and mathematics to understand nature.
- State that the Scientific Revolution began around 1600 and continued through the 1700s.
- Identify key figures in the Scientific Revolution (Harvey, Hooke, Leeuwenhoek, Descartes, Newton, Franklin) and their contributions.
- Explain that people gained confidence in their ability to understand the laws of nature.
- Define *modern* as meaning "of recent times."
- Explain that for historians "the modern world" means the world since the 1600s.
- Name some characteristics of the modern world, such as advances in medicine, health, communication, transportation, democracy, free speech, and space travel.
- Recognize the Scientific Revolution as the period beginning in 1600 when thinkers began to use experimentation, observation, and mathematics to understand the workings of nature.
- Interpret historical maps to gain information.

PREPARE

Approximate lesson time is 60 minutes.

Materials

    For the Student

        Understanding Geography: Map Skills and Our World (Level 4)

        History Journal

Lesson Notes

The student will be assessed on the historical maps in the next lesson, after completing the rest of the activity in the *Understanding Geography* book.

Keywords and Pronunciation

Scientific Revolution : A time of great progress in science. The Scientific Revolution began in the 1600s.

TEACH
Activity 1: The Scientific Revolution (Online)
Instructions
If your student has had the K12 third grade history program, or another systematic program such as the Core Knowledge Sequence, the following "Get Ready" should be a welcome and straightforward review. If your student has not had such a course, you may wish to skip the Get Ready and go directly to the lesson text. Or you may prepare for this lesson by using some of the online introductory lessons available in the earlier lesson titled Maps and Globes: Directions and Hemispheres.

Activity 2: History Journal (Offline)
Instructions
Print the Student Instructions and follow the directions to complete the activity.

Sample paragraph:

In history, the modern world began around the year 1600. That's when the Scientific Revolution began, too. People began to experiment. They observed things and wrote down their conclusions. They used math to figure out their results. They learned a lot of new things about nature.

Activity 3: Then and Now (Offline)
Instructions
This is another opportunity for the student to compare the modern world with the past.

Activity 4: Focus on Geography (Offline)
Instructions
Print the Student Instructions and follow the directions to complete the activity.

Understanding Geography Answers:

1. Cartier, Cortés, Ponce de León, Columbus (You only have to name two.)
2. Cartier started in France.
3. Vespucci explored the northern coast of South America.
4. Cortés entered Mexico.
5. Maine, Massachusetts, New Hampshire, Vermont, New York, Pennsylvania, Maryland, Virginia, North Carolina, Georgia (You only have to name four.)
6. Rhode Island, Connecticut, New Jersey, Delaware, South Carolina (You only have to name two.)
7. Massachusetts controlled the territory.
8. The British controlled the territory to the west and south.
9. Vermont

ASSESS

Lesson Assessment: What's So Modern About the Modern World? (Online)
Students will complete an online assessment based on the lesson objectives. The assessment will be scored by the computer. The attached answer key is the most current and may not coincide with previously printed guides.

Learning Coach Guide
Lesson 2: William Harvey Gets to the Heart of Things

William Harvey, an English physician, was the first to show how blood circulates in mammals. He discovered that the heart works like a pump, forcing blood to flow through arteries to the body and through veins back to the heart. His pathbreaking work became the basis for understanding the human heart and blood vessels.

Lesson Objectives

- Clearly explain in complete sentences that William Harvey was an English physician who discovered that blood circulates.
- Explain that William Harvey discovered the heart works like a pump to circulate blood.
- State that William Harvey used the scientific method.
- Interpret historical maps to gain information.

PREPARE

Approximate lesson time is 60 minutes.

Materials

> For the Student
>> History Journal
>> Understanding Geography: Map Skills and Our World (Level 4)

Lesson Notes

William Harvey (1578-1657) was the physician to James I and Charles I. He published his key work, *On the Motion of the Heart and Blood*, in 1628. His ideas were not fully accepted until after his death.

Keywords and Pronunciation

arteries : vessels that carry blood away from the heart.

blood vessels : Tiny pipes through which blood flows in the human body. Two kinds of blood vessels are arteries and veins.

cadavers (kuh-DA-vurs)

historical map : Map that tells about events that happened in the past.

scientific method : A way to find answers by experimenting, observing, and drawing conclusions.

veins : vessels that carry blood toward the heart

TEACH
Activity 1: In Circulation *(Online)*

Instructions

By reading an imaginary lecture delivered by William Harvey, the student learns how amazing Harvey's ideas were. Harvey's explanations of how the heart and the circulatory system worked were very different from the commonly held beliefs of most doctors of the times.

Activity 2: History Journal *(Offline)*
Instructions
Print the Student Instructions and follow the directions to complete the activity.

Activity 3: Reporting on a Remarkable Discovery *(Offline)*
Instructions
Print the Student Instructions and follow the directions to complete the activity.

Activity 4: Focus on Geography *(Offline)*
Instructions
Print the Student Instructions and follow the directions to complete the activity.

Answers to Activity 12: Historical Maps (continued)

10. southern Europe
11. 1348
12. 1350
13. yes
14. 1349
15. Mexico
16. Mexico, Belize, Guatemala, El Salvador (You only have to name three.)
17. It was the capital of the Aztec Empire.
18. Maya
19. Mexico

Skill Builder

1. Political maps show countries, states and their borders, cities, and capitals. Physical maps show landforms, relief, mountains, and bodies of water (they may not show political borders, which are established by people). Historical maps show events that happened in the past or historical places.

2. Historical maps can show the routes of explorers, the spread of people and diseases, and old and modern borders of states or countries. (You only have to mention two types of information.)

ASSESS

Lesson Assessment: William Harvey Gets to the Heart of Things, Part 1

(*Online*)

Students will complete an online assessment based on the lesson objectives. The assessment will be scored by the computer. The attached answer key is the most current and may not coincide with previously printed guides.

Lesson Assessment: William Harvey Gets to the Heart of Things, Part 2

(*Online*)

Use the answer key to evaluate your students' essay and input the total point value in the assessment. The attached answer key is the most current and may not coincide with previously printed guides.

TEACH

Activity 5. Optional: William Harvey Gets to the Heart of Things *(Online)*

Instructions

Print the Student Instructions and follow the directions to complete the activity.

Lesson Assessment Answer Key

William Harvey Gets to the Heart of Things, Part 2

Answers:

Answers will vary. Use the following grading rubric to award points for this question:

Did your student's article describe William Harvey as an English physician who had new ideas about the circulation of blood?	10 points
Did your student's article explain that William Harvey thought the heart worked like a pump?	10 points
Did your student's article explain that William Harvey experimented and drew conclusions from the results?	10 points
Did your student's article explain the audience reaction to William Harvey's ideas?	10 points
Did your student use complete sentences with clearly explained thoughts?	10 points

Learning Coach Guide
Lesson 3: What's Under That Microscope?

Just as Galileo made advances in astronomy by studying stars through a telescope, Robert Hooke and Anton van Leeuwenhoek made huge strides in biology by using early microscopes.

Lesson Objectives

- Describe the microscope as an important invention that helped scientists understand small life forms.
- State that Robert Hooke used an early form of the microscope.
- Describe Anton van Leeuwenhoek as one of the first people to record observations of microscopic life.
- Identify major physical features on the Earth.
- Use a landform map to identify physical features.

PREPARE

Approximate lesson time is 60 minutes.

Materials

For the Student

History Journal

Understanding Geography: Map Skills and Our World (Level 4)

Lesson Notes

Robert Hooke (1635-1703) was an English experimental scientist. Anton van Leeuwenhoek (1632-1723) was a Dutch amateur scientist who made microscopes that could magnify objects up to 270 times.

Keywords and Pronunciation

adapt : To change or adjust your life to fit the world around you.

animalcules (a-nuh-MAL-kyools) : Anton van Leeuwenhoek´s term for tiny organisms. It means "little animals".

Anton van Leeuwenhoek (AHN-tohn vahn LAY-ven-hook)

cape : A part of the land that sticks into the sea.

coastal plain : A flat area between ocean and higher land.

hill : A raised area on Earth, not as high as a mountain.

landform : A physical feature on the Earth, such as a mountain, hill, or island.

lens : A piece of clear glass with curved surfaces that can make an image look larger.

mountain : The tallest type of landform, higher than a hill.

peninsula : A body of land that sticks out and is almost completely surrounded by water.

piedmont : An area of land at the foot of a mountain range.

plain : An area of mostly flat land.

plateau (pla-TOH) : An area of high, flat land.

TEACH
Activity 1: Leeuwenhoek Takes a Closer Look (Online)
Instructions
This main teaching activity is online. Your student may want to complete this activity himself, or you may want to join him at the computer.

Activity 2: History Journal (Offline)
Instructions
With your student, read the History Journal entry for today's lesson and compare it with the sample paragraph below. Did it include the most important parts of the lesson?

Anton van Leeuwenhoek was a curious man who became a scientist. He was a cloth merchant, but he loved science. He made a microscope. It magnified things more than 200 times. He studied things that could not be seen by the naked eye. He observed lake water, spittle, and blood. He also observed tiny animals. Leeuwenhoek wrote down what he saw. He even had people draw pictures of the things he observed. He wrote to scientists and told them about his observations. Leeuwenhoek was a great scientist who studied microscopic things.

Activity 3: Focus on Geography (Online)
Instructions
Have your student:
- Read and discuss pages 30–33 of Understanding Geography, Activity 6, "Landforms."
- Answer Questions 1–17 in her History Journal.
- When your student has finished, she should compare her answers to the ones below.

Answers
Activity 6: Landforms
1. They are both flat, but a plateau is higher.
2. They are both bodies of land that jut into a body of water, but a peninsula is larger and is almost entirely surrounded by water.
3. You would find a piedmont at the bottom of a mountain range.
4. valley
5. hills
6. peninsula
7. piedmont
8. coastal plain
9. mountain
10. There are more mountains near the coast.
11. western
12. eastern
13. mountains or hills
14. hills
15. plains
16. hills
17. plains

ASSESS

Lesson Assessment: What's Under That Microscope? (*Online*)

Students will complete an online assessment based on the lesson objectives. The assessment will be scored by the computer. The attached answer key is the most current and may not coincide with previously printed guides.

TEACH

Activity 4. Optional: What's Under the Microscope (*Online*)

Instructions

In this optional activity, your student is asked to research how a microscope works and present an illustrated oral report.

Learning Coach Guide
Lesson 4: A Fly on the Ceiling: The Story of Cartesian Coordinates

René Descartes was a French mathematician and philosopher. His system of Cartesian coordinates helped mathematicians locate and describe objects, and made it possible to plot courses with greater precision.

Lesson Objectives

- Identify René Descartes as a French mathematician and philosopher.
- Describe Cartesian coordinates as a way of locating any object on a graph.
- Explain that Descartes's system was a great advance in mathematics.
- Use a map to identify physical features.

PREPARE

Approximate lesson time is 60 minutes.

Materials

> For the Student
>> Understanding Geography: Map Skills and Our World (Level 4)
>> History Journal

Lesson Notes

René Descartes (1596-1650) was a contemporary of Galileo. His key work was *Discourse on the Method of Rightly Conducting One's Reason and Seeking Truth in the Sciences* (1637).

Keywords and Pronunciation

Anton van Leeuwenhoek (AHN-tohn vahn LAY-ven-hook)

archipelago (ahr-kuh-PEH-luh-goh) : A group of islands in a large body of water.

Cartesian (kahr-TEE-zhuhn)

island : Land that is completely surrounded by water.

isthmus (IS-muhs) : A narrow piece of land that connects to larger land areas.

René Descartes (ruh-NAY day-KAHRT)

TEACH
Activity 1: Descartes and Cartesian Coordinates *(Online)*
Instructions

This main teaching activity is online. Your student may complete this activity alone or with your help.

Activity 2: History Journal *(Offline)*

Instructions

Read your student's History Journal entry for today's lesson. You will use the History Journal to assess his understanding of this lesson.

Answers:

1. René Descartes was a French mathematician and philosopher.
2. René Descartes invented the *x-y* system. It is also known as the Cartesian coordinate system.
3. Descartes's invention is used to locate an object on a graph.

Activity 3: Using Cartesian Coordinates *(Online)*

Instructions

This activity reinforces the concept of the Cartesian coordinate system. Your student will plot points on an online interactive graph.

Activity 4: Focus on Geography *(Online)*

Instructions

What does the land look like where you live? The physical features of the Earth vary from place to place. To learn more about landforms have your student:

- Read and discuss pages 34–35 of Activity 6, "Landforms," in *Understanding Geography*.
- Answer Questions 18–25 in her History Journal.
- When she has finished, have your student compare her answers to the ones below.

Answers

1. In the western part of the state there are many mountains. In the central part of the state you will find the piedmont. In the eastern part of the state you find the coastal plains.
2. You would expect to find them in the western or central part.
3. Charlotte, Winston-Salem, Greensboro, Durham, Raleigh (You only have to name three.)
4. You would expect to see mountains around Asheville.
5. You will find a cape on the coastal plain. Cape Hatteras, Cape Lookout, Cape Fear (You only need to name two.)
6. piedmont
7. Sumatra, Java, Borneo, Sulawesi, New Guinea (You only need to name two.)
8. The Panama Canal connects the Caribbean Sea and the Pacific Ocean.

ASSESS

Lesson Assessment: The Fly on the Ceiling: The Story of Cartesian Coordinates, Part 1 *(Online)*

Students will complete an online assessment based on the lesson objectives. The assessment will be scored by the computer. The attached answer key is the most current and may not coincide with previously printed guides.

Lesson Assessment: The Fly on the Ceiling: The Story of Cartesian Coordinates, Part 2 (*Offline*)

Review your student's responses in the History Journal activity and input the results online. The attached answer key is the most current and may not coincide with previously printed guides.

TEACH
Activity 5. Optional: A Fly on the Ceiling: The Story of Cartesian Coordinates
(*Online*)
Instructions
In this optional online activity, your student will visit a website where he can play a game in which he plots points using the Cartesian coordinate system.

Lesson Assessment Answer Key

A Fly on the Ceiling: The Story of Cartesian Coordinates, Part 2

Answers:

1. René Descartes was a French mathematician and philosopher.
2. René Descartes invented the *x-y* system. It is also known as the Cartesian coordinate system.
3. Descartes's invention is used to locate an object on a graph.

Learning Coach Guide
Lesson 5: Young Isaac Newton

An inquisitive and observant child, Isaac Newton spent long hours studying nature, building machines, and thinking about how the world worked. His interests were numerous. As a young man, he experimented with light and optics and puzzled over gravity.

Lesson Objectives

- Identify Isaac Newton as a great English scientist.
- Describe Newton as an observant and curious child.
- Tell about one of young Isaac Newton's experiments.
- Identify and distinguish different kinds of bodies of water.
- Identify and locate bodies of water on maps.
- Identify and define the source and mouth of rivers.

PREPARE

Approximate lesson time is 60 minutes.

Materials

For the Student

📖 Newton Apple Mobile, Part 1

Understanding Geography: Map Skills and Our World (Level 4)

History Journal

Lesson Notes

There is no formal assessment for today's lesson. The assessment at the end of the next lesson will cover both today's lesson and the next lesson.

Isaac Newton lived from 1642 to 1727.

Keywords and Pronunciation

Anton van Leeuwenhoek (AHN-tohn vahn LAY-ven-hook)

bay : A small body of water partly surrounded by land; usually smaller than a gulf.

fjord (fee-AWRD) : A narrow inlet from the sea between cliffs.

gulf : A part of a sea or ocean that extends into the land; usually larger than a bay.

lake : A body of water, usually freshwater, surrounded by land on all sides.

mouth : The end of a river, where it flows into a larger body of water.

ocean : One of four large bodies of salt water on Earth.

René Descartes (ruh-NAY day-KAHRT)

river : A large stream of freshwater that flows over land.

sea : A body of salt water that is smaller than an ocean.

source : The beginning of a river.

strait (strayt) : A narrow body of water connecting two larger bodies of water.

TEACH
Activity 1: Young Isaac Newton (Online)
Instructions
This main teaching activity is online. Your student may want to complete this activity by herself, or you may want to join her at the computer.

Activity 2: History Journal (Offline)
Instructions
With your student, read the History Journal entry for today's lesson and compare it with the sample paragraph below. Did it include the most important parts of the lesson?

Isaac Newton was a curious and observant child. He spent a lot of time alone doing experiments. He kept careful notes about the observations he made during his experiments. He was a student at the university in Cambridge, but he came home when the plague closed the school. One of his experiments was using a piece of glass to make a rainbow. Young Isaac Newton often thought about how the world around him worked.

Activity 3: Newton Apple Mobile (Online)
Instructions
This is the first part of a two-part activity. The second half appears in the next lesson. The activity involves creating a mobile that documents important events in Isaac Newton's life.

The following are examples of what your student should have included:

Newton as a Young Boy (about 1651): Newton was a curious child. He experimented with sundials. He recorded what he observed in a notebook.

Newton Returns Home from Cambridge (about 1661): Newton went to Cambridge University. Then the school closed because of the plague. He had to come home.

Newton Studies Light in the Study (about 1665): Newton experimented with light. He wondered if white light was really white. He got really involved in his experiments. Sometimes he even forgot to eat and sleep!

Activity 4: Focus on Geography (Online)
Instructions
Water covers nearly three-quarters of our planet. To learn more about bodies of water, have your student:

- Read and discuss pages 36–37 of Activity 7, "Bodies of Water", in *Understanding Geography*.
- Answer Questions 1–14 in her History Journal
- When she has finished, have your student compare her answers with the ones below.

Your student will be assessed on this geography information after she has completed "Bodies of Water" in the next lesson.

Answers
Activity 7, "Bodies of Water"

1. A bay is usually smaller than a gulf.
2. The water in a lake is fresh and the water in the ocean is salty.
3. Atlantic, Pacific, Indian, Arctic
4. The rivers in Europe include the Loire, Rhine, Oder, Danube, Dniester, Dnieper, Volga, and Ural. (You only have to name two.)
5. Atlantic Ocean
6. Arctic Ocean
7. Mediterranean Sea
8. Gulf of Bothnia
9. Lake Ladoga
10. North Sea
11. Black Sea
12. The Volga and the Ural flow into the Caspian Sea.
13. The Loire flows into the Bay of Biscay.
14. The Strait of Gibraltar separates the Iberian Peninsula from Africa.

Activity 5. Optional: Young Isaac Newton *(Online)*
Instructions

As a young man, Isaac Newton experimented with sundials. In this optional online activity, your student will visit the *Exploratorium* website and learn to make a "sun clock" of her own.

Learning Coach Guide
Lesson 6: A New Kind of Knight

Isaac Newton's pathbreaking work on gravity and motion changed the way people looked at the world. People began to think of the universe as orderly, regular, and governed by simple laws. They came to believe that human reason could decipher the laws of nature. Newton was knighted for his huge intellectual strides.

Lesson Objectives

- Recognize that Isaac Newton discovered laws of gravity and motion.
- Explain that because of Newton's work, people began to think of the universe as a place that followed basic laws of nature.
- Explain that Newton's work gave people confidence that they could understand how the universe worked if they experimented, observed things closely, and thought carefully.
- Identify and distinguish different kinds of bodies of water.
- Define source and mouth of a river.
- Identify and locate bodies of water on maps.
- Demonstrate mastery of knowledge and skills from previous lessons.

PREPARE

Approximate lesson time is 60 minutes.

Materials

For the Student

  🖥 Newton Apple Mobile, Part 2

  scissors, round-end safety

  Understanding Geography: Map Skills and Our World (Level 4)

  History Journal

Lesson Notes

Newton was knighted in 1705.

Keywords and Pronunciation

bay : A small body of water partly surrounded by land; usually smaller than a gulf.

fjord (fee-AWRD) : A narrow inlet from the sea between cliffs.

gravity : The force that pulls objects toward the Earth. It also keeps planets in orbit around the sun.

gulf : A part of a sea or ocean that extends into the land; usually larger than a bay.

lake : A large body of water, usually fresh, surrounded by land.

mouth : The end of a river, where it flows into a larger body of water.

ocean : One of four large bodies of salt water on Earth.

Principia (prin-SIH-pee-uh)

river : A large stream of freshwater that flows over land.

sea : A body of salt water that is smaller than an ocean.

source : The beginning of a river.

spectrum : A band of different colors formed when white light is separated by a prism. The spectrum has the same colors as a rainbow.

strait (strayt) : A narrow body of water connecting two larger bodies of water.

TEACH

Activity 1: Newton Is Knighted *(Online)*

Activity 2: History Journal *(Offline)*

Instructions

With your student, read the History Journal entry for today's lesson and compare it with the sample paragraph below. Did it include the most important parts of the lesson?

Isaac Newton's work gave people hope. At first, Newton kept his discoveries to himself. These discoveries included gravity and a new kind of math. He wrote a letter to another scientist about how gravity affects the planets. Then he wrote a book called *Principia.* He became famous and was knighted by the queen of England. His discoveries gave people hope. People started to believe that the universe was an orderly place that followed certain laws. They thought that if they observed things carefully, they could learn more. Sir Isaac Newton's observations and discoveries gave the world confidence.

Activity 3: Newton Apple Mobile *(Online)*

Instructions

This is the second part of a two-part activity. The first part appeared in the last lesson. The activity involves creating a mobile that documents important events in Isaac Newton's life.

The following are examples of what your student should include:

Newton as a Young Professor (about 1669): Newton went back to Cambridge and became a professor. He wrote to scientists and told them that white light is a mix of all the colors. People started to realize he was a genius.

Newton Discusses Planets with Visiting Scientist (about 1684): A scientist visited Newton and asked about the planets and the sun. Newton found the notes he had written about gravity. He wrote a letter to the scientist that explained gravity.

Newton Knighted by the Queen (1705): Newton had become famous for his work. The queen of England made him a knight. His discoveries gave people hope.

Activity 4: Focus on Geography *(Online)*

Instructions

China is a vast country with many bodies of water. To find out about them, have your student:

- Finish Activity 7, "Bodies of Water," by reading pages 38–39 of *Understanding Geography*.
- Answer Questions 15–24 in your History Journal.
- If you have time, you may want to answer the Skill Builder Questions on page 39. They are optional.
- When she has finished, have your student compare her answers with the ones below.

Answers

Activity 7, "Bodies of Water" (continued)

1. Yellow River
2. The Yellow Sea, East China Sea, Sea of Japan are east of China; the South China Sea is southeast of China. (You only have to name two.)
3. The Xi flows into the South China Sea.
4. Poyang Lake, Dongting Lake, Qinghai Lake (You only have to name one.)
5. Taiwan Strait
6. Korea Bay
7. The Sea of Japan separates China from Japan.
8. The South China Sea separates China from the Philippines.
9. Gulf of Tonkin
10. A = bay
    B = source
    C = lake
    D = mouth
    Optional

Skill Builder

1. source
2. strait
3. lake
4. Indian Ocean
5. Amazon River
6. Hudson Bay, Caribbean Sea, Bering Sea, Gulf of Mexico or Gulf of Alaska
7. Nile River

Try It Yourself

The Mississippi River flows through Minnesota, Wisconsin, Iowa, Illinois, Missouri, Kentucky, Tennessee, Arkansas, Mississippi, and Louisiana.

ASSESS

Lesson Assessment: A New Kind of Knight (*Online*)

Students will complete an online assessment based on the lesson objectives. The assessment will be scored by the computer. The attached answer key is the most current and may not coincide with previously printed guides.

TEACH
Activity 5. Optional: A New Kind of Knight (*Online*)

Learning Coach Guide
Lesson 7: Curious Ben Franklin

An American who was widely revered in Europe, Benjamin Franklin was a thinker and inventor as well as an important statesman. His curiosity, intelligence, and broad interests gave the world the lightning rod, bifocals, and the Franklin stove.

Lesson Objectives

- Describe Benjamin Franklin as a scientist and inventor with many interests.
- Explain that Benjamin Franklin conducted experiments on electricity and proved that lightning is really electricity.
- List some of Benjamin Franklin's inventions (lightning rod, bifocals, Franklin stove).

PREPARE

Approximate lesson time is 60 minutes.

Lesson Notes

Benjamin Franklin lived from 1706 to 1790.

Franklin was lucky to survive his kite experiment, which he carried out in 1752. The lightning could have killed him. In fact, another scientist died while testing Franklin's ideas.

You will need to assess your student's performance in the History Journal activity.

Keywords and Pronunciation

Anton van Leeuwenhoek (AHN-tohn vahn LAY-ven-hook)

Principia (prin-SIH-pee-uh)

TEACH
Activity 1: Scientific Revolutionary *(Online)*
Instructions

This lesson describes Benjamin Franklin's scientific efforts, especially his experiments with electricity. Be sure to caution your student about these experiments. Future lessons will focus on Franklin's efforts as a statesman.

Activity 2: History Journal *(Online)*
Instructions

With your student, read the History Journal entry for today's lesson and compare it with the answers presented here.

You will use the History Journal to assess her understanding of this lesson.

Answers

The six terms that apply to Franklin are:

key, kite, lightning rod, bifocals, electricity, and stove.

The following sentences are correct:

Benjamin Franklin was an inventor and a scientist with many interests.

Answers

The six terms that apply to Franklin are:

key, kite, lightning rod, bifocals, electricity, and stove.

The following sentences are correct:

Benjamin Franklin was an inventor and a scientist with many interests.

Benjamin Franklin conducted experiments on electricity and proved that lightning was really electricity.

Activity 3. Optional: Curious Ben Franklin (Online)

Instructions

The website in this activity is part of the larger website of the Franklin Institute. You may also want to explore the many other features available there.

Learning Coach Guide
Lesson 8. Optional: Diderot's Revolutionary Encyclopedia

The Age of Reason and the Scientific Revolution prompted thinkers to learn more about their world. But how could human beings gather and record that knowledge? Between 1751 and 1772, Frenchman Denis Diderot published a 28-volume encyclopedia that compiled current knowledge and thought. It was revolutionary in its scope and ideas.

Lesson Objectives

- Identify Denis Diderot as a man in love with ideas and knowledge.
- Describe Diderot as the editor of the first modern encyclopedia.
- Explain that the encyclopedia helped spread ideas and knowledge about science.
- Explain that the encyclopedia encouraged people to ask questions and think for themselves.
- Demonstrate mastery of important knowledge and skills taught in this lesson.

PREPARE

Approximate lesson time is 60 minutes.

Lesson Notes

You will use the student's writing from the History Journal and Write an Encyclopedia Article on Diderot activities for the lesson assessment.

Keywords and Pronunciation

Denis Diderot (duh-nee DEE-duh-roh)

TEACH
Activity 1. Optional: Optional Lesson Instructions *(Online)*

Activity 2. Optional: Diderot Organizes Everything *(Online)*

Activity 3. Optional: History Journal *(Offline)*

Instructions

Read your student's History Journal entry for today's lesson. The question is "What were the main effects of the publication of Diderot's encyclopedia?"
You will use this writing to assess your student's understanding of today's lesson. Compare the answer to this sample response:

Diderot's encyclopedia helped spread ideas and knowledge about science. It also got people to ask questions. It got them to think for themselves.

Activity 4. Optional: Write an Encyclopedia Article on Diderot *(Online)*
Instructions
Your student should complete this activity in the History Journal.

Activity 5. Optional: Diderot's Revolutionary Encyclopedia *(Online)*
Instructions
In this optional activity, your student will select and research a topic and write an encyclopedia article on that topic.

Learning Coach Guide
Lesson 9: Unit Review and Assessment

The student will review this unit and take the unit assessment.

Lesson Objectives

- Demonstrate mastery of important knowledge and skills in this unit.
- Express or identify a location using longitude and latitude.
- Recognize the Scientific Revolution as the period beginning in 1600 when thinkers began to use experimentation, observation, and mathematics to understand the workings of nature.
- Explain that William Harvey discovered the heart works like a pump to circulate blood.
- Describe the microscope as an important invention that helped scientists understand small life forms.
- Describe Anton van Leeuwenhoek as one of the first people to record observations of microscopic life.
- Identify René Descartes as a French mathematician and philosopher.
- Describe Newton as an observant and curious child.
- Recognize that Isaac Newton discovered laws of gravity and motion.
- Explain that Newton's work gave people confidence that they could understand how the universe worked if they experimented, observed things closely, and thought carefully.
- Explain that Benjamin Franklin conducted experiments on electricity and proved that lightning is really electricity.
- List some of Benjamin Franklin's inventions (lightning rod, bifocals, Franklin stove).
- Use a landform map to identify physical features.
- Describe the Scientific Revolution as a time of great progress in understanding nature.
- State that the Scientific Revolution began around 1600 and continued through the 1700s.
- Explain that people gained confidence in their ability to understand the laws of nature.

PREPARE

Approximate lesson time is 60 minutes.

TEACH
Activity 1: Introducing the Modern World: The Scientific Revolution (Offline)
Instructions

Print the Student Instructions and follow the directions to complete the activity.

Answers:

[1] about 1600

[2] that blood circulates

[3] It pumps blood.

[4] bacteria and things invisible to the eye

[5] He wrote down his results.

[6] Descartes

[7] how to locate things on a graph

[8] Isaac Newton

[9] that lightning is electricity

[10] the Franklin stove

[11] published an encyclopedia

Activity 2: History Journal Review (Offline)

Instructions

Print the Student Instructions and follow the directions to complete the activity.

Activity 3: Online Interactive Review (Online)

Instructions

The student will continue reviewing the unit by completing an online, interactive review.

ASSESS

Unit Assessment: Introducing the Modern World: The Scientific Revolution

(Online)

Students will complete an online assessment of the objectives covered so far in this unit. The assessment will be scored by the computer. The attached answer key is the most current and may not coincide with previously printed guides.

Learning Coach Guide
Lesson 1: John Locke Spells Out the Laws of Good Government

At a time when the first real scientists were making strides toward understanding the laws of nature, John Locke tried to figure out the laws of good government. In the wake of England's Glorious Revolution, he defended the rights of the people. His ideas would inspire British colonists in North America.

Lesson Objectives

- Name the American and French Revolutions as two great democratic revolutions.
- Describe the growing importance of ideas about inalienable rights, the right of revolution, and leaders deriving power from the people.
- Describe a constitution as the basic law of government, which sets up the form of the government.
- Recognize that the U.S. Constitution employs three branches of government and a system of checks and balances.
- Describe three stages of the French Revolution (monarchy, republic, empire).
- Describe the Terror as a time of violence when many "enemies of the revolution" were killed.
- Explain that the French Revolution led to major European wars.
- Identify key figures, documents, and events in the American and French Revolutions (John Locke, Thomas Jefferson, James Madison, George Washington, Lafayette, Louis XVI, Robespierre, Napoleon, the Declaration of Independence, the U.S. Constitution, storming the Bastille, the Napoleonic Code, Waterloo).
- Describe John Locke as an English political philosopher.
- Explain that Locke taught that everyone has rights, and that rulers must follow important laws of good government.
- Explain that Locke believed the power to rule a nation came from the nation's people.
- Explain that Locke believed that if rulers governed badly, the people had a right of revolution.
- Use relief maps to identify and compare elevations of selected locations.
- Explain that elevation is height above sea level.

PREPARE

Approximate lesson time is 60 minutes.

Materials

For the Student

    Understanding Geography: Map Skills and Our World (Level 4)

    History Journal

Lesson Notes

Instead of writing a History Journal entry for today's lesson, your student will write a letter in the A Letter About Locke activity. The student should write this activity in the History Journal. You will also use this activity as the lesson assessment.

John Locke lived from 1632 to 1704.

We advise that before beginning this lesson, students review the lesson on the Glorious Revolution. This is available as one of several introductory lessons from third grade.

Keywords and Pronunciation

elevation : The height of the land above sea level, also called *altitude*.

Glorious Revolution : A bloodless transfer of power to William and Mary in England. It established that Parliament was supreme.

philosopher : A person who seeks wisdom.

relief map : A map that shows the higher and lower parts of an area.

sea level : The level of the ocean; the elevation at sea level is 0 feet.

Thames (temz)

TEACH
Activity 1: The Right of Revolution *(Online)*

Activity 2: A Letter About Locke *(Offline)*
Instructions

The student should write this activity in the History Journal. You will use this activity to assess your student's understanding of today's lesson.

Activity 3: Focus on Geography *(Online)*
Instructions

Do you live at sea level or high up in the mountains? Relief maps can help you figure out the elevation of your region. How high up you live really influences the weather in your area. Today we'll take a look at how elevation affects climate.

- Begin Activity 8, "Elevation and Relief Maps," by reading and discussing pages 40–41 of *Understanding Geography*
- Have your student answer Questions 1–7 in his History Journal.
- When he has finished, your student should compare his answers to the ones below.
- Your student will be assessed on this geography information when he finishes Activity 8 in the next lesson.

Answers

Activity 8: Elevation and Relief Maps

1. Sacramento is less than 1,000 feet above sea level.
2. Susanville
3. It flows west (or southwest) because rivers flow from higher elevation to lower elevation.
4. Mount Whitney is above 10,000 feet.
5. Yreka
6. Sacramento Valley, San Joaquin Valley, Death Valley, Imperial Valley (You only have to name three.)
7. Mojave Desert

ASSESS

Lesson Assessment: John Locke Spells Out the Laws of Good Government

(*Online*)

Use the answer key to evaluate your students' essay and input the total point value in the assessment. The attached answer key is the most current and may not coincide with previously printed guides.

Lesson Assessment Answer Key

John Locke Spells Out the Laws of Good Government

Answers:

Answer will vary but should include to following five points. Use the grading rubric below to score this question.

- John Locke was an English political philosopher (or John Locke was an Englishman who thought about how government should work).
- Locke believed that everyone has rights.
- Locke believed that rulers must follow important laws of good government.
- Locke believed that the power to rule a nation comes from the nation's people.
- Locke believed that if rulers governed badly, the people have a right of revolution.

Score one point for each of the items above that your student included in the letter and reward points as described below:

four or five points	10 points
three points	8 points
two points	6 points
one point	4 points

Learning Coach Guide
Lesson 2: Thomas Jefferson and the Declaration of Independence

The imaginary conversation between Thomas Jefferson and Benjamin Franklin is intended to help your student understand more about John Locke's influence on the key ideas contained in the Declaration of Independence.

Lesson Objectives

- Explain that Americans defended their right of revolution using some of John Locke's ideas.
- Identify Thomas Jefferson as the author of the Declaration of Independence.
- Recognize that the words "we hold these truths to be self-evident, that all men are created equal" come from the Declaration of Independence.
- State that the United States became a republic.
- Use relief maps to identify and compare elevations of selected locations.
- Explain that elevation is height above sea level.

PREPARE

Approximate lesson time is 60 minutes.

Materials

For the Student

Understanding Geography: Map Skills and Our World (Level 4)

History Journal

Lesson Notes

In the K12 history program students study the development of colonies and the American Revolution in both third and fifth grades. This lesson briefly revisits the key ideas behind the American Revolution, which led to the first modern republican experiment.

For background on the British colonies in North America, see E.D. Hirsch Jr., *What Your Third Grader Needs to Know*, Revised Edition (New York: Doubleday, 2001), pp. 140-160. For solid background on the American Revolution, see E.D. Hirsch Jr., ed., *What Your First Grader Needs to Know*, Revised Edition (New York: Doubleday, 1997), pp. 158-171. (Even though the book is called *What Your First Grader Needs to Know*, the presentation on the American Revolution is suitable for fourth graders as well.) We advise reading these materials before this lesson if your student has not had the third grade K12 program.

Keywords and Pronunciation

delegate (DEH li guht) : A representative to a convention or conference.

elevation : The height of the land above sea level, also called *altitude*.

independence : Freedom from control by others.

relief map : A map that shows the higher and lower parts of an area.

republic : A government in which citizens elect representatives to govern according to laws.

sea level : The level of the ocean; the elevation at sea level is 0 feet.

self-evident : Obvious; clear and not needing proof.

tyrant : A ruler who has total power over people.

unalienable (uhn-AYL-yuh-nuh-buhl) : "Unalienable rights" are rights that cannot be taken away.

TEACH
Activity 1: Independence Declared! (Online)
Instructions
This activity features an imaginary conversation between Thomas Jefferson and Benjamin Franklin. It illustrates the influence of John Locke's ideas on the Declaration of Independence.

Activity 2: History Journal (Offline)
Instructions
This activity will serve as the assessment for the history portion of this lesson. Your student should copy and complete the questions in the History Journal. The answers will be available for you in the assessment section. The assessment section also includes some online questions about geography that your student should answer.

Activity 3: Focus on Geography (Offline)
Instructions
Thomas Jefferson was a statesman, a thinker, and a writer. And he was much more than that. He was a Renaissance man like Leonardo da Vinci. While he worked on the Declaration of Independence, Jefferson also kept careful records of the weather. When he became president and doubled the size of the country by buying land from the French, he quickly sent explorers to gather information about the new land. Today your student will explore the elevation of the United States. Have him:

- Read pages 42-43 of Activity 8, "Elevation and Relief Maps"
- Answer Questions 8–15 in his History Journal
- If he has time, he may want to answer the Skill Builder Questions on page 43. They are optional.
- When your student has finished, have him compare his answers with the ones below.

Answers

Activity 8: Elevation and Relief Maps (continued)
1. the West
2. You would travel to a higher elevation.
3. The Rio Grande flows southeast. Rivers flow from higher elevations into larger bodies of water at lower elevations.
4. The Missouri flows southeast. You can tell because rivers flow from higher elevations to lower elevations.
5. Miami, Houston, Raleigh, San Francisco, and Seattle (You only have to name two).
6. Mt. Whitney reaches 14,494 ft; Death Valley is 282 ft below sea level (-282 ft).
7. True
8. B, A, C

Skill Builder

1. A relief map shows the elevation of the land—the higher and lower parts of an area.
2. True
3. California has both low and very high elevations (it can be warm at the low elevations and snowing at the higher elevations at the same time).
4. Answers will vary. See map on page 42.
5. the southeast

ASSESS

Lesson Assessment: Thomas Jefferson and the Declaration of Independence, Part 1 (*Online*)

Students will complete an online assessment based on the lesson objectives. The assessment will be scored by the computer. The attached answer key is the most current and may not coincide with previously printed guides.

Lesson Assessment: Thomas Jefferson and the Declaration of Independence, Part 2 (*Online*)

Students will complete an offline assessment based on the lesson objectives. Print the assessment and have students complete it on their own. Use the answer key to score the assessment, and then enter the results online. The attached answer key is the most current and may not coincide with previously printed guides.

TEACH

Activity 4. Optional: Thomas Jefferson and the Declaration of Independence

(*Online*)

Instructions

This activity allows students to see Thomas Jefferson's rough draft, his lap desk, and other pictures related to the writing of the Declaration of Independence. Then they can "sign" a copy online.

Lesson Assessment Answer Key

Thomas Jefferson and the Declaration of Independence, Part 2

Answers:

1. John Locke
2. Declaration of Independence
3. self-evident
4. equal
5. republic

Learning Coach Guide
Lesson 3: James Madison and the U.S. Constitution

This lesson focuses on James Madison and the creation of the U.S. Constitution. It explores the issues under consideration in the development of this document. Two lessons follow on the workings of the government following ratification of the constitution.

Lesson Objectives
- Describe James Madison as the Father of the Constitution.
- Define *federal government* as a central government over all the states.
- Explain that James Madison studied history and knew that democracies usually didn't last long.
- Identify the Constitutional Convention as the meeting in which the United States made a new plan of government.
- Locate and identify major mountain ranges around the world.
- Identify selected mountain peaks.

PREPARE

Approximate lesson time is 60 minutes.

Materials
For the Student
>   glue, children's white non-toxic
>   paper, 8 1/2" x 11"
>   pencils, colored, 16 colors or more
>   scissors, round-end safety
>   Understanding Geography: Map Skills and Our World (Level 4)
>   History Journal

Keywords and Pronunciation
constitution (kahn-stuh-TOO-shuhn) : A document listing the powers and duties of a government.
delegate (DEH li guht) : A representative to a convention or conference.
mountain range : A large group of mountains.
physical map : A map showing the Earth's natural features, such as rivers, lakes, and mountains.

TEACH
Activity 1: A New Government *(Online)*

Instructions
This activity includes an imaginary discussion between James Madison, Edmund Randolph, and an unidentified New Yorker. It shows that many factors, including a careful study of historical precedents, went into creating a balanced government with three branches.

Activity 2: History Journal (Offline)

Instructions

Read your student's History Journal entry for today's lesson. Use this to informally assess your student's understanding of the lesson. The following sample paragraph shows the main ideas from the lesson. Compare your student's paragraph with the one below. Did your student include the most important parts of the lesson?

Read your student's History Journal entry for today's lesson. Use this to informally assess your student's understanding of the lesson. The following sample paragraph shows the main ideas from the lesson. Compare your student's paragraph with the one below. Did your student include the most important parts of the lesson?

Sample written narration: "James Madison was the Father of the Constitution. He studied governments from history and thought about the best one for the United States. The states sent delegates to a Constitutional Convention. James Madison helped them decide on the best way to have a government."

Activity 3: A Home Page for James Madison (Online)

Instructions

This activity requires a visit to the website of James Madison's home, Montpelier. After investigating this site, your student will design a web page to reflect Madison's role as Father of the Constitution.

Activity 4: Focus on Geography (Offline)

Instructions

There are mountains on every continent. To learn about some of the major mountain ranges around the world, have your student:

- Read page 44 of Activity 9, "Mountains," in *Understanding Geography*
- Answer Questions 1–11 in his History Journal.
- When he has finished, your student should compare his answers with the ones below.
- Your student will be assessed on this geography information after he has finished Activity 9 in the next lesson.

Answers

Activity 9: Mountains

1. South America
2. Europe
3. Asia
4. Europe and Asia
5. Africa
6. Rocky Mountains
7. Andes
8. Africa
9. Australia
10. Himalaya
11. North America

ASSESS

Lesson Assessment: James Madison and the U.S. Constitution (*Offline*)

Students will complete an online assessment based on the lesson objectives. The assessment will be scored by the computer. The attached answer key is the most current and may not coincide with previously printed guides.

TEACH

Activity 5. Optional: James Madison and the U.S. Constitution (Online)

Instructions

Visit these websites together to learn more about the U.S. Constitution.

Learning Coach Guide
Lesson 4: George Washington and the American Presidency

The first great test of the U.S. Constitution came in 1789, when George Washington was inaugurated as president. The American people loved Washington, but could a president become a king? What did it mean to be the president of the United States?

Lesson Objectives

- Explain that many Americans feared their strong president might become a king.
- Describe George Washington as a leader Americans trusted.
- Name two ways that George Washington helped put people's fears to rest (clothing, manners, title, stepping down after two terms).
- Locate and identify major mountain ranges around the world.
- Identify selected mountain peaks.
- Describe how people adapt to living in mountainous regions.

PREPARE

Approximate lesson time is 60 minutes.

Materials

> For the Student
>> Understanding Geography: Map Skills and Our World (Level 4)
>> History Journal

Lesson Notes

Many historians have described George Washington (1732-1799) as "the indispensable man." Without his wise leadership, it is not clear whether the American experiment with republican government would have succeeded.

Keywords and Pronunciation

mountain range : A large group of mountains.

physical map : A map showing the Earth's natural features, such as rivers, lakes, and mountains.

TEACH
Activity 1: The First President of the United States *(Online)*

Instructions

This main teaching activity is online. Your student may complete this activity alone or with your help.

Review the Show You Know questions carefully with your student to be sure the important difference between being king and being president is clear.

Activity 2: History Journal (Online)

Instructions

Read the History Journal entry for today's lesson. The following sample paragraph shows the main ideas from the lesson. Compare your student's paragraph with the one below. Are the most important parts of the lesson included?

The people of the United States didn't want a president who would try to become king. They trusted George Washington. He dressed in simple clothes. He told people to call him "Mr. President," not "Your Excellency" or "Your Highness." Washington retired after two terms as president. He didn't want people to think the president was becoming like a king.

Activity 3: The Many Jobs of the President (Online)

Instructions

This activity requires some time on the Internet. Be sure to review and monitor your student's work. You may need additional materials to create an object or artwork that illustrates one of the many jobs of the president.

Activity 4: Focus on Geography (Offline)

Instructions

To explore the mountains in France and learn how people adapt to living in the mountains have your student:

- Read pages 45–47 of Activity 9, "Mountains," in Understanding Geography
- Answer Questions 12–16 in his History Journal.
- If your student has time, he may want to answer the Skill Builder Questions on page 47. They are optional.
- When he has finished, your student should compare his answers with the ones below.

Answers

Activity 9: Mountains

1. the southeast
2. Lyons
3. Pyrenees
4. Nice
5. Alps

Skill Builder

1. Appalachian Mountains and Rocky Mountains
2. Alps
3. Andes
4. Africa, Asia, North America, and South America
5. Ural Mountains
6. The Appalachians have rounded tops and the Tetons have jagged, pointy peaks.
7. People can adapt to life in the mountains by wearing warm clothing, building secure shelters, and raising crops and animals well-suited to mountain life. (You only need to name two.)

ASSESS

Lesson Assessment: George Washington and the American Presidency

(*Online*)

Students will complete an online assessment based on the lesson objectives. The assessment will be scored by the computer. The attached answer key is the most current and may not coincide with previously printed guides.

Learning Coach Guide
Lesson 5: The U.S. Constitution: Three Branches of Government

The framers of the U.S. Constitution created a republic that divided power among three different branches of government. Each of those branches--legislative, executive, and judicial--has its own functions and powers.

Lesson Objectives

- Explain that the U.S. Constitution established rules for a government over all the states.
- State that the Constitution divides power among three branches of government.
- Name and describe at least one power of each of the three branches of government.

PREPARE

Approximate lesson time is 60 minutes.

Materials

> For the Student
>
> > The U.S. Constitution and You by Syl Sobel
> >
> > 💻 The Three Branches of Government activity sheet
> >
> > 💻 The Three Branches of Government answer sheet

Lesson Notes

The lessons on James Madison and the Constitution, and George Washington and the presidency, present much of the same material covered by the introduction in Syl Sobel's *The U.S. Constitution and You,* pages 6-10. The book's introduction provides good review and reinforcement for those lessons if needed.

Keywords and Pronunciation

branch of government : One part of the government.

executive branch : The branch of government that carries out the laws. The president is the head of the executive branch.

judicial branch : The branch of government that explains the laws and settles disagreements about them. The judicial branch includes the Supreme Court and other federal courts.

legislative branch : The branch of government that makes the laws. It includes Congress, which is made up of the Senate and the House of Representatives.

TEACH
Activity 1: The Three Branches of Government *(Online)*

Instructions

Your student will be reading *The U.S. Constitution and You,* pages 11 through 18, during this lesson. Feel free to have the student begin by reading pages 6 through 10, which review the background for the framing of the Constitution.

Activity 2: History Journal *(Online)*

Instructions

Read the History Journal entry for today's lesson. The following sample paragraph shows the main ideas from the lesson. Compare your student's paragraph with the one below. Did it include the most important parts of the lesson?

The federal government of the United States is divided into three branches. The legislative branch makes laws. The executive branch carries out the laws. The judicial branch decides what the laws mean. The Constitution set up these three branches of government.

Activity 3: The Three Branches of Government *(Offline)*

Instructions

The Three Branches of Government activity sheet should serve as a reference to help your student recall the important elements of each branch. An answer key is included so that either you or your student can check the work.

Activity 4. Optional: The U.S. Constitution: Three Branches of Government

(Online)

Instructions

Ben's Guide to U.S. Government is a comprehensive website that offers different information and activities for different grade levels. You may want to explore it in depth so that you can direct your student to other areas as well as those referenced here.

ASSESS

Lesson Assessment: The U.S. Constitution: Three Branches of Government

(Online)

Students will complete an online assessment based on the lesson objectives. The assessment will be scored by the computer. The attached answer key is the most current and may not coincide with previously printed guides.

Name

Date

The Three Branches of Government

Use the word bank to label the parts or people in each of the three branches of government.
There are more words in the bank than you will need, so choose carefully.

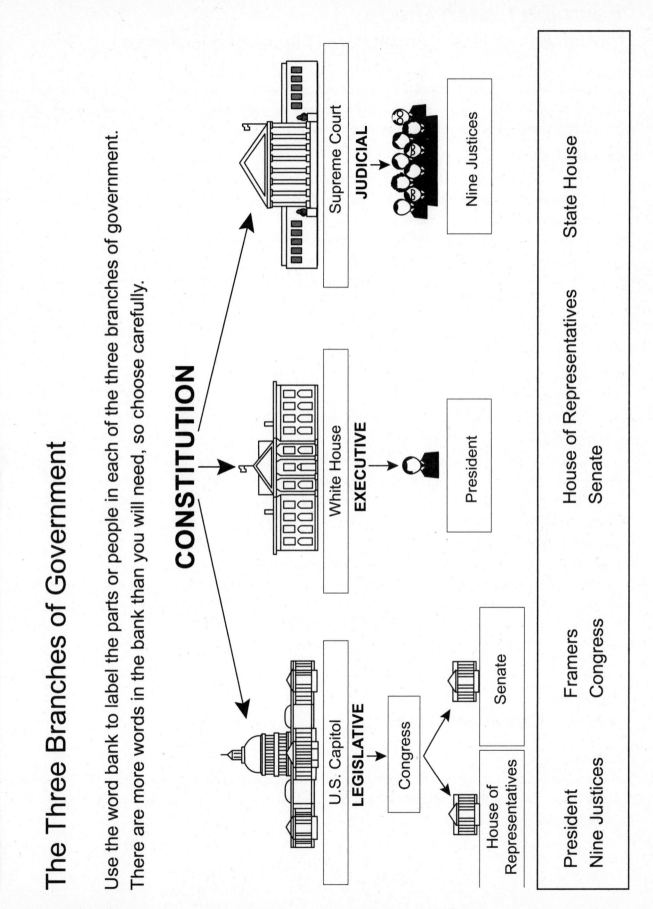

CONSTITUTION

Supreme Court

JUDICIAL

Nine Justices

White House

EXECUTIVE

President

U.S. Capitol

LEGISLATIVE

Congress

Senate

House of Representatives

House of Representatives   State House

Senate

Framers   President

Congress   Nine Justices

Learning Coach Guide
Lesson 6: The U.S. Constitution: Checks and Balances

Each branch of the U.S. government has some power over the others. This system of checks and balances ensures that no part of the government becomes supreme over the others. The Constitution establishes these checks. The Constitution can only be changed by amendment.

Lesson Objectives

- Define *checks and balances* as powers each branch of government has over the others.
- Name one check that the president has over Congress, that Congress has over the president, and that the Supreme Court has over Congress.
- Define *veto* as a presidential power to reject a law passed by Congress.
- Explain that the Constitution can only be changed by amendment.

PREPARE

Approximate lesson time is 60 minutes.

Materials

> For the Student
>
> > The U.S. Constitution and You by Syl Sobel

Lesson Notes

K12 students will study the Constitution and the history of the early republic in depth in fifth grade. We present a basic overview in these lessons. Although time does not allow this program to cover the entire book *The U.S. Constitution and You,* you may wish to read it with your student, particularly the excellent closing chapter "The Constitution and You."

Keywords and Pronunciation

amendment : A change; for example, a change to the Constitution.

checks and balances : Powers each branch of government has to control or limit the power of another branch of government.

impeach : To charge a government official with doing wrong.

veto : The presidential power to reject a law passed by Congress.

TEACH
Activity 1: Checks and Balances *(Online)*

Instructions

Your student will be reading *The U.S. Constitution and You,* pages 19 through 21 and pages 24 through 28, during this lesson. Feel free to have the student read the rest of the book, especially the section titled "The Constitution and You."

Activity 2: History Journal *(Online)*
Instructions
Read the History Journal entry for today's lesson. The following sample paragraph shows the main ideas from the lesson. Compare your student's paragraph with the one below. Did it include the most important parts of the lesson?

Checks and balances are powers that the branches of government have over each other. That way no branch can take control. A veto is an example of checks and balances. The president can veto a law that Congress makes. This means that Congress can't gain all the power in the government. Neither can the president or the courts.

Activity 3: Checks or Balances? *(Online)*
Instructions
This online interactive activity will help the student review and understand how the branches of government affect each other. You may use it several times or just once.

Activity 4. Optional: The U.S. Constitution: Checks and Balances *(Online)*
Instructions
This activity calls for a joint reading of the Bill of Rights. Although these are stated in a somewhat complicated way in the Constitution, they are explained succinctly on page 28 of Syl Sobel's *The U.S. Constitution and You.* Review them and compare them together with the original document.

ASSESS

Lesson Assessment: The U.S. Constitution: Checks and Balances (*Online*)
Students will complete an online assessment based on the lesson objectives. The assessment will be scored by the computer. The attached answer key is the most current and may not coincide with previously printed guides

Learning Coach Guide
Lesson 7: Rumblings of Revolution in France

Democratic ideals soon spread to France, a country ruled by a powerful king. The French Revolution began when Louis XVI called together the Estates General. The people demanded a constitution for France.

Lesson Objectives

- Identify Louis XVI as the French king at the time of the French Revolution.
- Explain that French kings believed they ruled by divine right.
- Using complete sentences, explain that the French people were eager for a constitution that would give them a say in government.
- Identify the members of the Third Estate as people who were neither nobles nor clergy.

PREPARE

Approximate lesson time is 60 minutes.

Materials

For the Student

crayons, 64 colors or more

paper, 8 1/2" x 11"

pencils, colored, 16 colors or more

Lesson Notes

The Versailles Palace website listed here takes you to the home page. The links within the Beyond the Lesson activity take you directly to the information on Marie Antoinette and the Marquis de Lafayette referenced in the activity.

Keywords and Pronunciation

debt : Something owed.

Estates General : The French congress. It consisted of three different groups (estates).

Louis (LOO-ee)

Marie Antoinette (muh-REE an-twuh-NET)

Marquis de Lafayette (mahr-KEE duh lah-fee-ET)

oath (OHTH) : A promise.

philosophes (fee-luh-ZAWFS)

TEACH
Activity 1: Setting the Stage for Another Revolution *(Online)*

Instructions

This lesson introduces the seeds of the French Revolution. It includes an imaginary conversation between Thomas Jefferson and the Marquis de Lafayette. Lafayette had helped during the American Revolution. This main teaching activity is online. Your student may complete this activity alone or with your help.

Activity 2: A Session in Court (Online)
Instructions
This activity requires the student to look at a painting online and then create another version with a caption.

Activity 3: History Journal (Online)
Instructions
Read the History Journal entry for today's lesson. Use it to assess your student's understanding of the lesson. The following sample paragraph shows the main ideas from the lesson. Compare your student's paragraph with the one below. Did it include the most important parts of the lesson?

Louis XVI was the king of France. He believed that kings should rule by divine right. The clergy were the First Estate. The nobles were the Second Estate. The ordinary people belonged to the Third Estate. The French people wanted rights and a constitution. They wanted a say in the government, too.

Activity 4. Optional: Rumbling the Revolutions in France (Online)
Instructions
This online tour of Versailles Palace can be as extensive or as limited as you would like to make it.

ASSESS

Lesson Assessment: Rumblings of Revolution in France (Online)
Use the answer key to evaluate your students' essay and input the total point value in the assessment. The attached answer key is the most current and may not coincide with previously printed guides.

Lesson Assessment Answer Key

Rumblings of Revolution in France

Answers:

Answers will vary. Use the grading rubric below to award points for this question.

Did your student's journal entry identify Louis XVI as the French king at the time of the French Revolution?	10 pts.
Did your student explain that French kings believed they ruled by divine right?	10 pts.
Did your student explain that the French people were eager for a constitution that would give them a say in running the government?	10 pts.
Did your student describe the Third Estate?	10 pts.
Did your student use complete sentences in the journal entry?	10 pts.
Total:	

Learning Coach Guide
Lesson 8: Storming the Bastille!

Worried about the new National Assembly, Louis XVI readied troops in Paris. Parisians believed that arms were stored in the Bastille, a prison fortress. They stormed the Bastille on July 14, 1789. The French celebrate Bastille Day as a national holiday.

Lesson Objectives

- Identify the Bastille as a prison or fortress.
- Describe the Bastille as a hated symbol of royal power to many people in France.
- Explain that on July 14, 1789, a large crowd stormed the Bastille.
- Use complete sentences to explain that Bastille Day is a national holiday in France and is regarded as the start of the French Revolution.

PREPARE

Approximate lesson time is 60 minutes.

Materials

For the Student

paper, 8 1/2" x 11"

pencils, colored, 16 colors or more

Keywords and Pronunciation

Bastille (bah-STEEL) : A royal fortress in Paris.

Pierre (pee-EHR)

TEACH
Activity 1: The Revolution Takes to the Streets *(Online)*
Instructions

The storming of the Bastille is considered the start of the French Revolution. It led to the Declaration of the Rights of Man and ultimately to a constitution. It also set the stage for what happened to King Louis XVI and Marie Antoinette.

Activity 2: History Journal *(Offline)*
Instructions

With your student, read the History Journal entry for today's lesson and compare it with the sample paragraph. Did it include the most important parts of the lesson?

You will use the History Journal to assess the student's understanding of this lesson.

The Bastille was a prison in Paris. Many people in France hated it. It was a symbol of royal power. King Louis wanted the people to pay more taxes. The poor people were going hungry. They decided to attack the Bastille. A crowd stormed the Bastille and got inside on July 14, 1789. That day was the beginning of the French Revolution. Now people in France celebrate Bastille Day every July 14.

Activity 3: Storming the Bastille: A Day to Remember *(Online)*
Instructions
This is the first lesson asking your student to create a political cartoon. There is a sample in the activity, but you may want to provide some additional support.

Activity 4. Optional: Storming the Bastille *(Online)*
Instructions
This website offers the chance to learn more about French history and France today.

ASSESS
Lesson Assessment: Storming the Bastille! (*Online*)
Use the answer key to evaluate your students' essay and input the total point value in the assessment. The attached answer key is the most current and may not coincide with previously printed guides.

Lesson Assessment Answer Key

Storming the Bastille!

Answers:

Answers will vary. Use the grading rubric below to award points for this question.

Did your student identify the Bastille as a prison or fortress?	10 pts.
Did your student describe the Bastille as a hated symbol of royal power?	10 pts.
Did your student explain that on July 14, 1789, a large crowd stormed the Bastille?	10 pts.
Did your student explain that Bastille Day is a national holiday in France?	10 pts.
Did your student explain that Bastille Day is regarded as the start of the French Revolution?	10 pts.
Did your student use complete sentences in the paragraph?	10 pts.
Total:	

Learning Coach Guide
Lesson 9: Farewell, Louis: From Monarchy to Republic

The French Revolution brought a new constitution that limited the powers of the king, Louis XVI. When Louis and his wife, Marie Antoinette, tried to flee France, they were arrested and eventually beheaded. With its king gone, France became a republic.

Lesson Objectives

- Explain that Louis XVI was arrested and later beheaded.
- Describe Louis XVI as opposed to changes that limited the king's power.
- Explain that France changed from a monarchy to a republic.

PREPARE

Approximate lesson time is 60 minutes.

Materials

> For the Student
>> History Journal

Keywords and Pronunciation

constitution (kahn-stuh-TOO-shuhn) : A document listing the powers and duties of a government.

guillotine (GIH-luh-teen)

Marie Antoinette (muh-REE an-twuh-NET)

Vive la république (veev lah ray-poob-leek)

Vive le roi (veev luh rwa)

TEACH
Activity 1: King Louis XVI Loses His Head *(Online)*
Instructions

This lesson deals with the beheading of Louis XVI and Marie Antoinette. You may want to preview it to decide how much you will monitor or discuss it with your student.

Activity 2: Why Didn't Louis Last? *(Offline)*
Instructions

This activity presents ten statements--some true, some false--about the factors that caused the executions of Louis XVI and Marie Antoinette. Your student will choose the true statements and copy them into the History Journal.

Guided Learning: Check the sentences in your student's History Journal against the list that follows. (Statements 2, 6, 8, and 10 are false.)

1. Louis XVI didn't really accept the new French constitution.

3. Marie Antoinette insisted on bringing so many things that they were noticed.

4. Louis XVI and Marie Antoinette took their time leaving and traveled slowly.

5. Louis XVI opposed the changes that limited his power as king of France.

7. Louis XVI's picture was on some French money, so it was easy to recognize him.

9. Louis XVI tried to end the French Revolution by getting help from Austria.

Activity 3. Optional: Farewell, Louis: From Monarchy to Republican (Online)
Instructions
This optional activity takes the student to a website that offers a multimedia tour of the French Revolution.

ASSESS
Lesson Assessment: Farewell, Louis: From Monarchy to Republic (Online)
Students will complete an online assessment based on the lesson objectives. The assessment will be scored by the computer. The attached answer key is the most current and may not coincide with previously printed guides.

Learning Coach Guide
Lesson 10: The Terror!

After the execution of Louis XVI, the French Revolution moved into a period of terrible violence known as the Terror. Robespierre led the Committee of Public Safety, which came to govern France. It made frequent use of the guillotine. Many people lived in fear of their lives.

Lesson Objectives

- Describe Robespierre as a revolutionary leader in France.
- Explain that Robespierre and the Committee of Public Safety used terror against supporters of the king and "enemies of the Revolution."
- Use complete sentences to describe the Terror as a period of terrible revolutionary violence in which many people who opposed the Revolution were killed.

PREPARE

Approximate lesson time is 60 minutes.

Keywords and Pronunciation

Liberté, égalité, fraternité (lee-behr-TAY, ay-ga-lee-TAY, fra-tehr-nee-TAY)

Maximilien Robespierre (mahk-see-meel-yan ROHBZ-pyehr)

TEACH
Activity 1: Fear Grips France *(Online)*
Instructions

The information on Robespierre and the Terror requires adult participation. Many gruesome events were part of this period in French history.

Activity 2: History Journal *(Offline)*
Instructions

With your student, read the History Journal entry for today's lesson and compare it with the sample paragraph below. Did it include the most important parts of the lesson?

You will use the History Journal to assess the student's understanding of this lesson.

The French Revolution turned into a time called the Terror. The leader of the Terror was named Maximilian Robespierre. He was the head of the Committee of Public Safety. Robespierre saw enemies everywhere. His weapon was terror. He used the guillotine to kill enemies of the Revolution. He ruled through fear. No one was safe. Thousands of people had their heads cut off. Then the people of France grew tired of the Terror. They arrested Robespierre. They sent him to the guillotine. Finally the Terror was over.

Activity 3: Robespierre in Time *(Online)*

Instructions

This online activity involves clicking and dragging information about Robespierre to make a simple time line of his life.

ASSESS

Lesson Assessment: The Terror! (*Online*)

Use the answer key to evaluate your students' essay and input the total point value in the assessment. The attached answer key is the most current and may not coincide with previously printed guides.

TEACH

Activity 4. Optional: The Terror! *(Online)*

Instructions

During the Revolution, the French created a new calendar. It was a radical departure from the calendar we know. Join your student to visit the *French Revolutionary Calendar* website.

© 2013 K12 Inc. All rights reserved.
Copying or distributing without K12's written consent is prohibited.

Lesson Assessment Answer Key

The Terror!

Answers:

Answers will vary. Use the grading rubric below to award points for this question.

Did your student include, in some way, the fact that Robespierre was a revolutionary leader in France? *(10 points)*	
Did your student include, in some way, the fact that Robespierre and the Committee of Public Safety used terror against supporters of the king and "enemies of the Revolution"? *(10 points)*	
Did your student include, in some way, the fact that Terror was a period of violence? *(10 points)*	
Did your student include, in some way, the fact that many people were killed during the Terror? *(10 points)*	
Total:	

Learning Coach Guide
Lesson 11: The Rise of Napoleon

Napoleon Bonaparte started out as an ambitious young army officer with republican sympathies. He quickly rose to become a general and then the leader of France. Napoleon rose to the position of First Consul in 1799. He is still remembered as one of the greatest military minds in history.

Lesson Objectives

- Describe Napoleon as one of the greatest generals in history.
- Explain that Napoleon led French republican armies to victory in many parts of the world, and name two of these victories.
- Explain that military triumphs made Napoleon very popular in France.
- State that Napoleon became First Consul of France.

PREPARE

Approximate lesson time is 60 minutes.

Materials

For the Student

📇 Map of Napoleonic Europe

📇 Napoleon's Triumphs Activity Sheet

For the Adult

📇 Napoleon's Triumphs Answer Key

Keywords and Pronunciation

Attaque! Toujours l'attaque (uh-tahk! too-zhour lah-tahk!)

Corsica (KOR-sih-kuh)

Napoleon Bonaparte (nuh-POHL-yuhn BOH-nuh-pahrt)

Toulon (too-LAWN)

TEACH
Activity 1: France's Dashing Young General *(Online)*

Instructions

This main teaching activity explains how Napoleon Bonaparte becomes one of the greatest generals and conquerors in history. Your student may complete this activity alone or with your help.

Activity 2: History Journal (Offline)
Instructions
With your student, read the History Journal entry for today's lesson and compare it with the sample paragraph below. Did it include the most important parts of the lesson?

Napoleon Bonaparte was a great French general. He was from an island called Corsica. Napoleon wanted to be a general ever since he was a boy. He helped save Paris from some angry mobs. He led the French army against the enemies of France. He won battles in Austria and Egypt. The people of France were very proud of Napoleon because of his victories. He was so popular, he became the head of the new French government. He was called the First Consul. Napoleon became the most powerful man in France.

Activity 3: Napoleon's Triumphs (Online)
Instructions
The student will complete an activity sheet that shows how Napoleon led French republican armies to victory in many parts of the world. When your student finishes, check his work using the answer key.

ASSESS
Lesson Assessment: The Rise of Napoleon (Online)
Students will complete an online assessment based on the lesson objectives. The assessment will be scored by the computer. The attached answer key is the most current and may not coincide with previously printed guides.

TEACH
Activity 4. Optional: The Rise of Napoleon (Online)
Instructions
In this optional online activity, the student will put together jigsaw puzzles based on paintings of Bonaparte.

Lesson 11: Napoleon's Triumphs

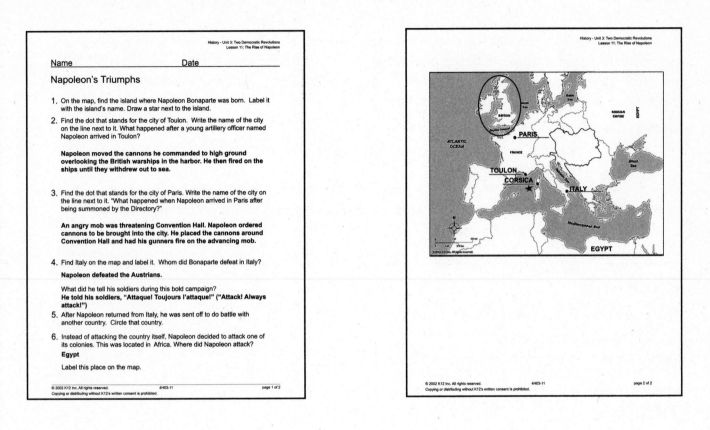

Name _____ Date _____

Napoleon's Triumphs

1. On the map, find the island where Napoleon Bonaparte was born. Label it with the island's name. Draw a star next to the island.

2. Find the dot that stands for the city of Toulon. Write the name of the city on the line next to it. What happened after a young artillery officer named Napoleon arrived in Toulon?

   Napoleon moved the cannons he commanded to high ground overlooking the British warships in the harbor. He then fired on the ships until they withdrew out to sea.

3. Find the dot that stands for the city of Paris. Write the name of the city on the line next to it. "What happened when Napoleon arrived in Paris after being summoned by the Directory?"

   An angry mob was threatening Convention Hall. Napoleon ordered cannons to be brought into the city. He placed the cannons around Convention Hall and had his gunners fire on the advancing mob.

4. Find Italy on the map and label it. Whom did Bonaparte defeat in Italy?

   Napoleon defeated the Austrians.

   What did he tell his soldiers during this bold campaign?
   He told his soldiers, "Attaque! Toujours l'attaque!" ("Attack! Always attack!")

5. After Napoleon returned from Italy, he was sent off to do battle with another country. Circle that country.

6. Instead of attacking the country itself, Napoleon decided to attack one of its colonies. This was located in Africa. Where did Napoleon attack?

   Egypt

   Label this place on the map.

4H03-11

page 1 of 2

4H03-11

page 2 of 2

73

Learning Coach Guide
Lesson 12. Optional: Washington's Farewell: Stay Out of Europe's Wars

Americans thought hard about how to respond to events in France. They were citizens of a nation born of democratic revolution. France had helped them in their own Revolutionary War. But George Washington said the United States should steer clear of alliances with foreign nations. He began what would become a long tradition of U.S. isolation from the affairs of countries in Europe.

Lesson Objectives

- Explain that some Americans wanted the United States to help the French in their war against the rest of Europe.
- Describe the Farewell Address as the speech George Washington wrote when he left office.
- Describe the Farewell Address as a speech that said Americans should protect their liberty by staying out of European wars.

PREPARE

Approximate lesson time is 60 minutes.

Keywords and Pronunciation

levee (LEH-vee) : A formal reception for state visitors.

TEACH
Activity 1. Optional: Optional Lesson Instructions *(Online)*

Activity 2. Optional: Washington Says Farewell *(Online)*
Instructions

This main teaching activity is online. Your student may complete this activity alone or with your help.

Activity 3. Optional: History Journal *(Offline)*
Instructions

With your student, read the History Journal entry for today's lesson and compare it with the sample paragraph below. Did it include the most important parts of the lesson?
You will use the History Journal to assess the student's understanding of this lesson.

George Washington wrote a famous speech called the Farewell Address. He wrote the speech when he was getting ready to leave office. Many Americans wanted to help the French Revolution. They wanted to help France fight its war in Europe. But George Washington said that the United States should stay out of the war. His Farwell Address told people that America should not fight so it could get strong. Some people did not like the Farewell Address. But the United States stayed out of Europe's wars. It followed George Washington's advice.

Activity 4. Optional: A Letter to the Editor *(Offline)*
Instructions
The student will write a letter to the editor of a Philadelphia newspaper in response to George Washington's farewell speech.

Activity 5. Optional: Washington's Farewell: Stay Out of Europe's Wars *(Offline)*
Instructions
The student will do some research to learn about the part of a president's administrative office organization called the cabinet.

Learning Coach Guide
Lesson 13: Napoleon: Lawgiver and Emperor

When Napoleon crowned himself "emperor of the French" in 1804, France moved from republic to empire. The French Revolution, which had begun with hopes for rule by the people, ended in rule by a single man. Yet Napoleon remained popular in France. He continued to stun and dismay the rest of Europe with his conquests.

Lesson Objectives

- Explain that, after years of revolution and violence, the French wanted a strong leader.
- Describe Napoleon as the republican hero who became an all-powerful emperor.
- Describe the Napoleonic Code as Napoleon's greatest accomplishment.

PREPARE

Approximate lesson time is 60 minutes.

Materials

For the Student

    📖 Bonaparte and Caesar activity sheet

    What's the Deal? Jefferson, Napoleon, and the Louisiana Purchase by Rhoda Blumberg

Keywords and Pronunciation

code : A system of law.

Vive l'Empereur (veev lahng-pehr-ehr)

TEACH
Activity 1: The Emperor and Lawgiver *(Online)*
Instructions
This main teaching activity is online. Your student may complete this activity alone or with your help.

Activity 2: Napoleon Bonaparte and Julius Caesar, Part 1 *(Offline)*
Instructions
The student will research and take notes comparing and contrasting the empires and careers of Napoleon Bonaparte and Julius Caesar. This activity will be finished in the next lesson.

ASSESS

Lesson Assessment: Napoleon: Lawgiver and Emperor (*Online*)

Students will complete an offline assessment based on the lesson objectives. Print the assessment and have students complete it on their own. Use the answer key to score the assessment, and then enter the results online. The attached answer key is the most current and may not coincide with previously printed guides.

TEACH
Activity 3. Optional: Lawgiver and Emperor *(Offline)*
Instructions
In this optional offline activity, the student will learn about Napoleon's part in the Louisiana Purchase by reading *What's the Deal? Jefferson, Napoleon, and the Louisiana Purchase,* by Rhoda Blumberg (Washington: National Geographic Society, 1998).

Lesson Assessment Answer Key

Napoleon: Lawgiver and Emperor

Answers:

1. a strong leader
2. emperor
3. The Napoleonic Code was Napoleon's greatest accomplishment.

Learning Coach Guide
Lesson 14: Waterloo!

Napoleon's amazing conquests appalled Europe's kings and queens. Determined to end his reign, they sent armies after him. Even after they captured him, he escaped and returned to power. Finally, he met the Duke of Wellington at Waterloo. There Napoleon was defeated for good in one of the most famous battles of all time.

Lesson Objectives

- Explain that Napoleon had many conquests and built a vast empire.
- Identify Waterloo as the famous battle in which Napoleon was defeated.
- Identify the Duke of Wellington as the British hero who defeated Napoleon.
- Understand that the expression "meet your Waterloo" means to be defeated by something.

PREPARE

Approximate lesson time is 60 minutes.

Materials
> For the Student
>> 📖 Map of Napoleonic Europe

Keywords and Pronunciation
plateau (pla-TOH) : A flat stretch of high land.

Vive l'Empereur (veev lahng-pehr-ehr)

TEACH
Activity 1: Master of Europe *(Online)*
Instructions
This main teaching activity is online. Your student may complete this activity alone or with your help.

Activity 2: Napoleon Bonaparte and Julius Caesar *(Offline)*
Instructions
The student will complete the activity he started in the last lesson. In that lesson, he researched and took notes on the empires and careers of Napoleon Bonaparte and Julius Caesar. In this lesson, the student will write two paragraphs: one that compares and contrasts these two leaders' careers, and one that does the same for their empires.

ASSESS

Lesson Assessment: Waterloo! (*Offline*)

Students will complete an online assessment based on the lesson objectives. The assessment will be scored by the computer. The attached answer key is the most current and may not coincide with previously printed guides.

TEACH

Activity 3. Optional: Waterloo! (*Online*)

Instructions

In this optional online activity, the student can visit the St. Helena Official Tourist Site. He can also take on the role of Napoleon or Wellington in a decision-making game that can be found on the BBC website. The game is a little advanced and requires quite a bit of reading. If your student is going to play the game, you should join him at the computer.

Learning Coach Guide
Lesson 15: Unit Review and Assessment

The student will review this unit and take the unit assessment.

Lesson Objectives

- Demonstrate mastery of important knowledge and skills in this unit.
- Describe John Locke as an English political philosopher.
- Explain that Locke taught that everyone has rights, and that rulers must follow important laws of good government.
- Explain that Locke believed that if rulers governed badly, the people had a right of revolution.
- Identify Thomas Jefferson as the author of the Declaration of Independence.
- State that the United States became a republic.
- Describe James Madison as the Father of the Constitution.
- Identify the Constitutional Convention as the meeting in which the United States made a new plan of government.
- Explain that many Americans feared their strong president might become a king.
- State that the Constitution divides power among three branches of government.
- Name and describe at least one power of each of the three branches of government.
- Define *checks and balances* as powers each branch of government has over the others.
- Explain that the Constitution can only be changed by amendment.
- Identify Louis XVI as the French king at the time of the French Revolution.
- Describe Robespierre as a revolutionary leader in France.
- Explain that Robespierre and the Committee of Public Safety used terror against supporters of the king and "enemies of the Revolution."
- Describe Napoleon as one of the greatest generals in history.
- Describe Napoleon as the republican hero who became an all-powerful emperor.
- Describe the Napoleonic Code as Napoleon's greatest accomplishment.
- Identify the Duke of Wellington as the British hero who defeated Napoleon.
- Explain that on July 14, 1789, a large crowd stormed the Bastille.
- Name the American and French Revolutions as two great democratic revolutions.
- Describe a constitution as the basic law of government, which sets up the form of the government.
- Describe three stages of the French Revolution (monarchy, republic, empire).
- Describe the Terror as a time of violence when many "enemies of the revolution" were killed.
- Explain that the French Revolution led to major European wars.

PREPARE

Approximate lesson time is 60 minutes.

TEACH

Activity 1: Two Democratic Revolutions *(Offline)*

Instructions

The student will review this unit and take the unit assessment.

Answers

Activity 1

[1] Thomas Jefferson

[2] life, liberty, and the pursuit of happiness

[3] the Constitutional Convention

[4] James Madison

[5] legislative, executive, and judicial

[6] checks and balances

[7] the Third Estate

[8] The people of Paris stormed the Bastille.

[9] He was guillotined.

[10] The Terror

[11] Napoleon

[12] The Napoleonic Code

[13] the great battle in which the British defeated Napoleon

Activity 2: History Journal Review *(Offline)*

Instructions

The student will use the History Journal to review for the unit assessment. You can help by asking questions based on the work in the journal.

Activity 3: Online Interactive Review *(Online)*

Instructions

The student will continue reviewing the unit by completing an online, interactive review.

ASSESS

Unit Assessment: Two Democratic Revolutions (*Offline*)

Students will complete an offline Unit Assessment. Print the assessment and have students complete it on their own. Use the answer key to score the assessment, and then enter the results online. The attached answer key is the most current and may not coincide with previously printed guides.

Two Democratic Revolutions

Count ten points for each correct answer.

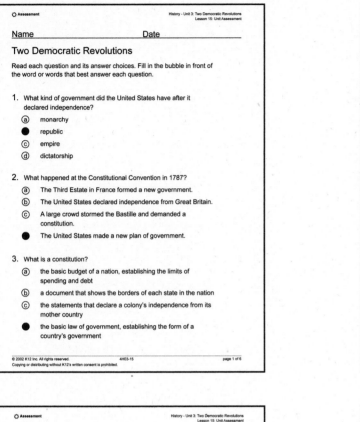

Two Democratic Revolutions

Match the name of each person on the left with a description of the person on the right. Write the letter of the description on the line in front of the name. (There is one extra description on the right that does not match any of the people on the left.)

14. **B** John Locke   A. British general who defeated Napoleon at Waterloo

    C Thomas Jefferson   B. English political philosopher who taught that everyone has rights

    F James Madison   C. Wrote the Declaration of Independence

    E Louis XVI   D. Great French general who became an all-powerful emperor

    G Robespierre   E. French king at the time of the French Revolution

    D Napoleon   F. Known as the Father of the Constitution

    A Duke of Wellington   G. Revolutionary leader in France who used terror against "enemies of the revolution"

    H. Revolutionary War hero and first president of the United States

15. Delegates who met in Philadelphia in 1787 for the Constitutional Convention had a big job to do. They had to write the basic law of government for their new nation. The result of their work was the U.S. Constitution.

Write a paragraph that:

· Explains what the U.S. Constitution is
· Names the three branches of government that the U.S. Constitution created
· Describes at least one power of each branch
· Explains how the U.S. Constitution keeps any one branch from gaining too much power

A topic sentence is provided, but you should end the paragraph with a concluding sentence.

Delegates met in Philadelphia, Pennsylvania, in 1787 and wrote a new constitution for the United States of America. _____

_____

_____

_____

_____

_____

_____

_____

_____

_____

_____

_____

Scoring the Essay Question

This essay question is worth eighty points. Score the student's writing as follows:

· ten points for explaining what the U.S. Constitution is (The U.S. Constitution is a document that establishes the form of government of the United States. It's the basic law of government for the country.)

· ten points for each branch of government that the Constitution created (legislative, executive, judicial), for a maximum of thirty points

· ten points for each power named (executive—veto bills, choose judges, carry out the laws, sign bills into law; legislative—make laws regulating trade among states, declare war, levy taxes, make a vetoed bill a law, impeach officials, approve judges; judicial—settle disagreements about the law, declare laws unconstitutional, judges serve for life), for a maximum of thirty points

· ten points for explaining how the U.S. Constitution keeps any one branch from gaining too much power (The U.S. Constitution created a system of checks and balances. These are rules that give each branch of government some power to control the power of the other branches.)

Learning Coach Guide
Lesson 1: Haiti Went First: Toussaint L'Ouverture

When the French recognized the "universal rights of man," it lit the torch of liberty in their own colonies. In 1791 Toussaint L'Ouverture, a former slave, led a revolution in the French colony of Saint Domingue. The colony gained its independence from France and became the country we know as Haiti.

Lesson Objectives

- Define Latin America.
- Describe the spread of democratic revolution to Latin America.
- Describe Haiti as the first black republic.
- Describe Spain as the major colonial power in Latin America.
- Recognize that a strong class system existed in the Spanish colonies, dividing the population into Spaniards, Creoles, mestizos, Indians, and sometimes slaves.
- Explain that Spain exercised strict control over colonial decisions and that colonists resented their lack of control.
- Locate major colonies-turned-nations on a map of Latin America (Mexico, Venezuela, Colombia, Peru, Bolivia, Argentina, Chile, Brazil).
- Identify key figures and events of major revolutions in Latin America (including Toussaint L'Ouverture, Francisco Miranda, Miguel Hidalgo, Simon Bolívar).
- Describe Saint Domingue as a French colony on the island of Hispaniola and locate it on a map.
- Explain that a large slave population existed on Hispaniola and that the slaves rebelled against their French masters.
- Identify Toussaint L'Ouverture as the leader of the revolution for Haitian independence.
- Describe Haiti as the first black republic.
- Distinguish between weather and climate.
- Describe the relation between latitude and climate.
- Distinguish between polar, temperate, and tropical climates.
- Analyze climate maps for information.

PREPARE

Approximate lesson time is 60 minutes.

Materials

For the Student

📖 Map of Europeans in the New World, 1800

Understanding Geography: Map Skills and Our World (Level 4)

History Journal

Lesson Notes

Toussaint L'Ouverture lived from about 1743 to 1803.

Keywords and Pronunciation

climate : The usual pattern of weather in a particular place over a very long period of time.

climate zone : area on earth that has similar temperature, rainfall, snowfall, and sunshine

Haiti (HAY-tee)

Hispaniola (his-puh-NYOH-luh)

revolution (re-vuh-LOO-shuhn) : the traveling of the Earth or another body around the sun; one complete revolution of the earth takes one year

rotation : The spinning of the Earth on its axis; one complete rotation takes one day.

Saint-Domingue (sehn-daw-MEHNG)

Toussaint L'Ouverture (too-SEHN loo-vair-tyour)

weather : The condition of the air at a particular moment of time.

TEACH
Activity 1: L'Ouverture Liberates Haiti (Online)
Instructions

This main teaching activity is online. Your student may complete this activity alone or with your help.

Activity 2: History Journal (Offline)
Instructions

With your student, read the History Journal entry for today's lesson and compare it with the sample paragraph below. Did it include the most important parts of the lesson?

Saint Domingue was a colony on the island of Hispaniola. It belonged to the French. There were many black slaves there. When the slaves heard about revolution in France, they wanted liberty. Toussaint L'Ouverture led the revolution. He died in France, but the people of Saint Domingue won their freedom. The country of Haiti became the first black republic.

Activity 3: Extra! Extra! Revolution in Haiti! (Offline)
Instructions

In this offline activity, your student will write a short newspaper article about the revolution in Haiti.

Activity 4: Focus on Geography (Online)
Instructions

What is the difference between weather and climate? To find out, have your student:

- Read pages 48–49 of Activity 10, "Weather and Climate," in *Understanding Geography*.
- Answer Questions 1–8 in her History Journal.
- When she has finished, have her compare her answers with the ones below.
- Your student will be assessed on this geography information after she finishes Activity 10 in the next lesson.

Answers

1. Answers may vary. The most likely response is temperate climate.
2. polar
3. tropical
4. Rome, Athens, Madrid (You only have to name two.)
5. cold
6. I would wear shorts and a T-shirt in Athens.
7. I would wear a sweater and heavy coat.
8. My friend will pack an umbrella because London has cool, wet summers.

ASSESS

Lesson Assessment: Haiti Went First: Toussaint L'Ouverture (*Offline*)

Students will complete an online assessment based on the lesson objectives. The assessment will be scored by the computer. The attached answer key is the most current and may not coincide with previously printed guides.

TEACH

Activity 5. Optional: Haiti Went First: Toussaint L'Ouverture (*Offline*)

Instructions

In this optional offline activity, your student will research the country of Haiti and write a short report.

Learning Coach Guide
Lesson 2: Spanish America and Seeds of Independence

Revolutionary movements in North America and France awakened similar stirrings for self-government in Latin America. There Spain ruled over a vast, tightly controlled empire, and colonists had begun to chafe at the bit.

Lesson Objectives

- Explain that in 1800 Spain ruled over most of Central and South America.
- Give one example of ways Spain kept tight control over the colonists (only Spaniards could rule; Spain decided all the American laws).
- Recognize that colonists had come to resent Spain's tight control.
- Explain that some colonists desired independence as they watched events in the young United States and in France.
- Distinguish between weather and climate.
- Describe the relation between latitude and climate.
- Distinguish between polar, temperate, and tropical climates.
- Analyze climate maps for information.
- Explain the relation between seasons in the Northern and Southern Hemispheres.

PREPARE

Approximate lesson time is 60 minutes.

Materials

> For the Student
>
> > 🖥 Map of Europeans in the New World, 1800
> >
> > Understanding Geography: Map Skills and Our World (Level 4)
> >
> > History Journal

Lesson Notes

Instead of writing a History Journal entry for today's lesson, your student will write an advertisement in the Miranda's Advertisement activity. The student should complete this activity in the History Journal. You will also use this activity as the lesson assessment.

K12 students study the Age of Exploration, along with Spanish and Portuguese colonization of the Americas, in the third grade. In this lesson we present a very brief review. For background reading, we suggest E.D. Hirsch, Jr. ed., *What Your First Grader Needs to Know*, Revised Edition (Doubleday, 1997), pages 135-147. For greater detail, read E.D. Hirsch, Jr., ed, *What Your Fifth Grader Needs to Know* (Doubleday, 1993), pages 107-116 and 119-126.

Keywords and Pronunciation

Chile (CHIH-lee)

climate : The usual pattern of weather in a particular place over a very long period of time.

climate zone : area on earth that has similar temperature, rainfall, snowfall, and sunshine

Francisco de Miranda (fran-SEES-koh day mee-RAHN-dah)

Latin America : The area of South, Central, and North America (except for Canada) originally colonized by Spain, Portugal, and France.

revolution (re-vuh-LOO-shuhn) : the traveling of the Earth or another body around the sun; one complete revolution of the earth takes one year

rotation : The spinning of the Earth on its axis; one complete rotation takes one day.

Venezuela (veh-nuh-ZWAY-luh)

weather : The condition of the air at a particular moment of time.

TEACH

Activity 1: Francisco Miranda Recruits *(Online)*

Instructions

This main teaching activity is online. Your student may complete this activity alone or with your help.

The activity includes an imaginary conversation with the revolutionary Francisco Miranda, who tried to free Venezuela from Spanish control in the early 1800s.

Activity 2: Miranda's Advertisement *(Online)*

Instructions

In this offline activity, your student will write Francisco Miranda's recruiting advertisement. You will use this activity to assess your student's understanding of the lesson.

Activity 3: Focus on Geography *(Online)*

Instructions

Why do we have seasons? To find out, have your student:

- Read pages 50–51 of Activity 10, "Weather and Climate," in *Understanding Geography*.
- Answer Questions 9–12 in her History Journal.
- If she has time, she may want to answer the Skill Builder Questions on page 51. They are optional.
- When she has finished, compare her answers with the ones below.

Answers

Activity 10: Weather and Climate

9. summer
10. Answers may vary. The most likely response is spring.
11. The Earth revolves around the sun and some parts of the Earth receive the suns rays more directly than other parts because the Earth is tilted on its axis.
12. The Northern Hemisphere gets more direct sunlight in June.

Skill Builder

1. Weather is the condition of the air at a particular moment in time. Climate is the usual pattern of weather over a very long period of time.
2. cooler
3. tropical climate
4. The climate of most of the United States is cooler than the climate of Africa. Africa is mostly in a tropical zone and the United States is mostly in a temperate zone.
5. away from the sun
6. fall
7. rotation, revolution

ASSESS

Lesson Assessment: Spanish America and Seeds of Independence, Part 1

(*Online*)

Students will complete an online assessment based on the lesson objectives. The assessment will be scored by the computer. The attached answer key is the most current and may not coincide with previously printed guides.

Lesson Assessment: Spanish America and Seeds of Independence, Part 2

(*Offline*)

Use the answer key to evaluate your students' essay and input the total point value in the assessment. The attached answer key is the most current and may not coincide with previously printed guides.

TEACH

Activity 4: Spanish America and Seeds of Independence (*Online*)

Lesson Assessment Answer Key

Spanish America and Seeds of Independence, Part 2

Answers:

Answers will vary. Use the grading rubric below to award points for this question.

Did your student's advertisement include the fact that in 1800 Spain ruled over most of Central and South America?	10 pts.
Did your students's advertisement point out that Spanish colonists in Central and South America resented Spain's tight control over their lives?	10 pts.
Did your students's advertisement state that some colonists wanted independence and were inspired by events in the United States and in France?	10 pts.
Did your student's advertisement give at least one example of how Spain tightly controlled her colonies?	10 pts.
Total:	

Learning Coach Guide
Lesson 3: Miguel Hidalgo: Father of Mexican Independence

When Napoleon invaded Spain, many colonists in Spanish America thought the time had come to rule themselves. In 1810 Father Miguel Hidalgo y Costilla, a priest born in Mexico, rallied his parishioners and started the Mexican war for independence.

Lesson Objectives

- Identify Miguel Hidalgo as a Mexican priest and the Father of Mexican Independence.
- Explain that Miguel Hidalgo called the people of Hidalgo's church together and urged them to rebel against Spain.
- State that Hidalgo's famous speech (*Grito de Dolores*) is read every year on Mexican Independence Day.
- Define and give examples of precipitation.
- Describe rain forests and deserts in terms of precipitation.
- Analyze precipitation maps and graphs for information on climate.

PREPARE

Approximate lesson time is 60 minutes.

Materials

For the Student

📖 Map of Europeans in the New World, 1800

Understanding Geography: Map Skills and Our World (Level 4)

History Journal

Keywords and Pronunciation

climograph : a special kind of graph that shows the average temperature and precipitation in a certain place during a year

creoles (KREE-ohls) : In the context of this lesson, people of Spanish descent who were born in the Spanish American colonies.

Dolores (doh-LOH-res)

eucalyp : A dry, often sandy area that gets very little rain.

Francisco de Miranda (fran-SEES-koh day mee-RAHN-dah)

Grito de Dolores (GREE-toh day doh-LOH-res)

mestizos (meh-STEE-zohs) : People with both Indian and Spanish ancestors.

Miguel Hidalgo (mee-GEHL ee-DAHL-goh)

precipitation : The moisture that falls to the Earth; rain, snow, sleet, and hail are all forms of precipitation.

rain forest : A densely wooded area that receives more than 100 inches of rain per year.

TEACH
Activity 1: The Cry of Dolores (Online)
Instructions
This main teaching activity is online. Your student may complete this activity alone or with your help.

Activity 2: History Journal (Online)
Instructions
Read the History Journal entry for today's lesson. The following sample paragraph shows the main ideas from the lesson. Compare your student's paragraph with the one below. Did it include the most important parts of the lesson?

Miguel Hidalgo was a Mexican priest. He is known as the Father of Mexican Independence. In the early 1800s, Mexico was called New Spain. It was ruled by Spain. Many of the people who lived in New Spain wanted independence from Spain. Indians who lived there were often treated badly. They were paid low wages. Father Hidalgo gave a speech in the town of Dolores. He urged them to rebel against Spain. For many years, Mexicans fought for their independence. By 1821, they were free of Spanish rule. Hidalgo's famous speech is read every year on Mexican Independence Day.

Activity 3: Grito de Dolores (Online)
Instructions
The student will write and give the speech that Father Miguel Hidalgo might have given in Dolores.

Activity 4: Focus on Geography (Online)
Instructions
What's the most significant difference between a desert and a rain forest? Rain. The amount of moisture an area receives determines what plants grow there. To learn more about climate and precipitation maps, have your student:

- Read pages 52–53 of Activity 11, "Climate and Precipitation," in *Understanding Geography*.
- Answer Questions 1–7 in her History Journal.
- When she has finished, have her compare her answers with the ones below.
- Your student will be assessed on this geography information after she finishes Activity 11 in the next lesson.

Answers
Activity 11: Climate and Precipitation
1. The Sahara is yellow and tan. It gets less than 4 inches (or 10 cm) of rain per year.
2. Kinshasa gets more than 40 inches (100 cm) of rain per year.
3. Tripoli receives between 10.1 and 20 inches of rain per year.
4. Nairobi receives between 20.1 and 40 inches of precipitation per year.
5. Mogadishu receives between 10.1 and 20 inches of rain per year.
6. Liberia receives more than 40 inches of rain per year.
7. No, because water is very scarce in the Sahara.

ASSESS
Lesson Assessment: Miguel Hidalgo: Father of Mexican Independence
(*Online*)

Students will complete an online assessment based on the lesson objectives. The assessment will be scored by the computer. The attached answer key is the most current and may not coincide with previously printed guides.

TEACH
Activity 5. Optional: Miguel Hidalgo: Father of Mexican Independence *(Online)*
Instructions

In this optional activity, your student is asked to research Cinco de Mayo (May 5). The student will write a short paragraph explaining this holiday's origins and how it differs from Mexican Independence Day (September 16).

Learning Coach Guide
Lesson 4: Simón Bolívar: The Liberator

Inspired by the American and French Revolutions, Caracas-born Simón Bolívar became the most important leader of Spanish American independence. His military triumphs won independence for Venezuela, Colombia, Ecuador, Peru, and Bolivia. He is known as "the Liberator" of South America.

Lesson Objectives

- Describe Simón Bolívar as a great South American revolutionary and general.
- Explain that Bolívar led military campaigns to free much of Spanish America and is known as "the Liberator."
- Name at least two areas that Bolívar liberated.
- Locate the areas Bolívar liberated (Venezuela, Colombia, Panama, Ecuador, Peru, and Bolivia) on a map of South America.
- Identify Bolivia as a country named for Bolívar.
- Define and give examples of precipitation.
- Describe rain forests and deserts in terms of precipitation.
- Analyze precipitation maps and graphs for information on climate.
- Use climographs to gain information.

PREPARE

Approximate lesson time is 60 minutes.

Materials

For the Student

- 🖥 Map of South America (Gran Colombia)
- 🖥 The Liberation of South America

  Understanding Geography: Map Skills and Our World (Level 4)

  History Journal

Lesson Notes

Bolívar lived from 1783 to 1830.

You will use the History Journal entry for today's lesson to assess your student's understanding of the lesson.

Keywords and Pronunciation

Caracas (kah-RAH-kahs)

climograph : a special kind of graph that shows the average temperature and precipitation in a certain place during a year

Creole (KREE-ohl) : In the context of this lesson, people of Spanish descent who were born in the Spanish-American colonies.

---

eucalyp : A dry, often sandy area that gets very little rain.

liberate : In the context of this lesson, to free from the control of a foreign power.

precipitation : The moisture that falls to the Earth; rain, snow, sleet, and hail are all forms of precipitation.

rain forest : A densely wooded area that receives more than 100 inches of rain per year.

Simón Bolívar (see-MOHN buh-LEE-vahr)

Venezuela (veh-nuh-ZWAY-luh)

TEACH
Activity 1: Bolívar Liberates South America *(Online)*
Instructions

This main teaching activity is online. Your student may complete this activity alone, or with your help.

Activity 2: History Journal *(Online)*
Instructions

Read your student's History Journal entry for today's lesson. Use it to assess her understanding of the lesson.

Here are sample answers:

1. Describe Simón Bolívar.
Simón Bolívar was a great South American revolutionary and general.
2. What is Bolívar known as?
Bolívar is known as "the Liberator."
3. What did he do?
He led military campaigns to free much of Spanish America.
4. Name at least two areas that Bolívar liberated (freed).
Bolívar liberated Venezuela, Colombia, Panama, Ecuador, Peru, and Bolivia. (The student should name at least two of these countries.)
5. What country was named for Simón Bolívar?
Bolivia was named for Simón Bolívar.

Activity 3: The Liberation of South America *(Offline)*
Instructions

In this map-based offline activity, your student will trace Bolívar's route and sequence the countries he liberated. You will need to save this activity sheet. The student will finish Part 2 in the next lesson.

Activity 4: Focus on Geography *(Online)*
Instructions

To learn more about climographs and the climate in Africa, have your student:

- Read pages 54–55 of Activity 11, "Climate and Precipitation," in *Understanding Geography.*
- Answer Questions 8–16 in her History Journal.
- When she has finished, she should compare her answers with the ones below.

Answers

Activity 11: Climate and Precipitation (continued)

1. Cairo, Egypt
2. June
3. Johannesburg gets approximately 7 inches of rain.
4. See the map on page 53.
5. Cairo
6. Cairo
7. Lagos
8. May, June, July
9. Nile River

Skill Builder

1. precipitation
2. rain forests
3. desert
4. precipitation (rainfall) and temperature

ASSESS

Lesson Assessment: Simón Bolívar: The Liberator, Part 1 (*Online*)

Students will complete an online assessment based on the lesson objectives. The assessment will be scored by the computer. The attached answer key is the most current and may not coincide with previously printed guides.

Lesson Assessment: Simon Bolivar - The Liberator, Part 2 (*Offline*)

Review your student's responses in the Show You Know: History Journal activity, and input the results online. The attached answer key is the most current and may not coincide with previously printed guides.

TEACH

Activity 5. Optional: Simon Bolivar: The Liberator (*Online*)

Instructions

In this optional activity, your student will research the country of Bolivia and give an illustrated oral presentation.

Lesson Assessment Answer Key

Simón Bolívar: The Liberator, Part 2

Answers:

1. Simón Bolívar was a great South American revolutionary and general.

2. Bolívar is known as "the Liberator."

3. He led military campaigns to free much of Spanish America.

4. Bolívar liberated Venezuela, Colombia, Panama, Ecuador, Peru, and Bolivia. (The student should name at least two of these countries.)

5. Bolivia was named for Simón Bolívar.

Learning Coach Guide
Lesson 5. Optional: Liberating the South: San Martín and O'Higgins

José de San Martín of Argentina and Bernardo O'Higgins of Chile are their countries' liberators and national heroes. San Martín led the fight for Argentine independence. Then he joined forces with O'Higgins. They crossed the Andes in 1817 with armies from both colonies, and went on to liberate Chile and Peru.

Lesson Objectives

- Identify José de San Martín and Bernardo O'Higgins as two great liberators of South America.
- Locate the Andes on a map.
- Describe the Army of the Andes as forces led by San Martín and O'Higgins that crossed the Andes mountain range.
- Explain that San Martín and O'Higgins liberated Chile.

PREPARE

Approximate lesson time is 60 minutes.

Materials

For the Student

   🖥 Map of South America, 1810 -1830

   map, world

   🖥 The Liberation of South America

For the Adult

   🖥 The Liberation of South America Answer Key

Keywords and Pronunciation

Andes (AN-deez)

Buenos Aires (BWAY-nuhs AIR-eez)

Ecuador (EH-kwuh-dor)

José de San Martín (hoh-SAY day san mahr-TEEN)

La Plata (lah PLAH-tah)

Lima (LEE-muh)

Paraguay (pah-rah-GWIY)

Uruguay (oo-roo-GWIY)

TEACH
Activity 1. Optional: Optional Lesson Instructions (Online)

Instructions

This lesson is OPTIONAL. It is provided for students who seek enrichment or extra practice. You may skip this lesson.

If you choose to skip this lesson, then go to the Plan or Lesson Lists page and mark this lesson "Skipped" in order to proceed to the next lesson in the course.

Activity 2. Optional: San Martín and O'Higgins Team Up *(Online)*
Instructions
This main teaching activity is online. Your student may complete this activity alone or with your help.

Activity 3. Optional: History Journal *(Offline)*
Instructions
With your student, read the History Journal entry for today's lesson and compare it with the sample paragraph below. Did it include the most important parts of the lesson?

San Martín was from La Plata in South America. He wanted to help free his country from the Spanish. He met Bernardo O'Higgins. Together they took an army called the Army of the Andes and crossed over the high mountains. It was a long, tough trip. They made it across, though. They fought the Spanish and drove them out of Chile. Then San Martín sailed to Peru and helped Bolívar beat the Spanish again. Finally South America was free from Spain.

Activity 4. Optional: The Liberation of South America *(Online)*
Instructions
Your student will complete the map-based offline activity begun in the lesson on Simón Bolívar. This activity requires the Liberation of South America activity sheet from that lesson. If the student does not have it, it can be printed again.

Activity 5. Optional: Liberating the South: San Martin and O'Higgins *(Offline)*
Instructions
In this optional offline activity, your student will compare the Andes with two other mountain ranges.

Name_____   Date_____

The Liberation of South America: Answer Key

Part 1

1. On the map, write "1" on the first country Bolívar liberated. Then label the country by writing its name on the line provided.

2. Starting from the first country, draw a solid black line with an arrow. It should point to the country he marched to and liberated next. Write "2" and the name of that country on the line.

3. Draw an arrow from the second country to the third country Bolívar liberated. Write "3" and the country's name on the line.

4. From the third country, draw an arrow to the fourth country he and his forces liberated. Write "4" and the country's name on the line.

5. These four smaller countries formed a new, independent country. What was its name? **Gran Colombia**

6. Who was elected president of this new country? **Simón Bolívar**

7. Draw an arrow from the fourth country to the fifth country Bolívar liberated. Write "5" and the country's name on the line.

8. Bolívar turned a section of the fifth country into a separate country. Write "6" and this country's name on the line provided. (Hint: The country named itself to honor Bolívar.)

The Liberation of South America: Answer Key

3. Panama

1. Venezuela

2. Colombia

4. Ecuador

5. Peru

6. Bolivia

7. Argentina

8. Chile

PACIFIC
OCEAN

ATLANTIC
OCEAN

Cartagena

Caracas

Bogotá

Quito

Amazon River

Lima

Buenos Aires
La Plata

Rio de
la Plata

N

0   500   1000 mi
0   500   1000 km

∧ Andes
   (Mountains)

The Liberation of South America: Answer Key

Part 2: Complete after the Liberating the South: San Martín and O'Higgins lesson.

1. Show the Andes mountain range on the map using this symbol: ^. Add this symbol to the map legend.

2. What two South American leaders combined forces to defeat the Spanish?

   José de San Martín

   Bernardo O'Higgins

3. On the map, write "7" and label the country where the Army of the Andes began its march.

4. Write "8" and label the country that the Army of the Andes marched to and liberated.

Learning Coach Guide
Lesson 6: Unit Review and Assessment

The student will review this unit and take the unit assessment.

Lesson Objectives

- Demonstrate mastery of important knowledge and skills in this unit.
- Demonstrate mastery of important knowledge and skills taught in previous lessons.
- Identify Toussaint L'Ouverture as the leader of the revolution for Haitian independence.
- Give one example of ways Spain kept tight control over the colonists (only Spaniards could rule; Spain decided all the American laws).
- Recognize that colonists had come to resent Spain's tight control.
- Explain that some colonists desired independence as they watched events in the young United States and in France.
- Identify Miguel Hidalgo as a Mexican priest and the Father of Mexican Independence.
- Explain that Bolívar led military campaigns to free much of Spanish America and is known as "the Liberator."
- Locate the areas Bolívar liberated (Venezuela, Colombia, Panama, Ecuador, Peru, and Bolivia) on a map of South America.
- Define Latin America.
- Describe Haiti as the first black republic.
- Describe Spain as the major colonial power in Latin America.
- Recognize that a strong class system existed in the Spanish colonies, dividing the population into Spaniards, Creoles, mestizos, Indians, and sometimes slaves.
- Explain that Spain exercised strict control over colonial decisions and that colonists resented their lack of control.

PREPARE

Approximate lesson time is 60 minutes.

TEACH
Activity 1: Latin American Revolutions (Offline)
Instructions
The student will review this unit and take the unit assessment.
Answers:

[1] Haiti

[2] Toussaint L'Ouverture

[3] France

[4] He was a slave.

[5] Spain

[6] Not well; the Spanish looked down on them.

[7] Spanish Americans had no say in how their country was run.

[8] Father Miguel Hidalgo

[9] Simón Bolívar

[10] Argentina

[11] Chile

[12] Bernardo O'Higgins

[13] Peru

[14] Brazil

Activity 2: History Journal Review (Offline)
Instructions
The student will use the History Journal to review for the unit assessment. You can help by asking questions based on the work in the journal.

Activity 3: Online Interactive Review (Online)
Instructions
The student will continue reviewing the unit by completing an online, interactive review.

ASSESS

Unit Assessment: Latin American Revolutions (Offline)
Students will complete an offline Unit Assessment. Print the assessment and have students complete it on their own. Use the answer key to score the assessment, and then enter the results online. The attached answer key is the most current and may not coincide with previously printed guides.

Latin American Revolutions

Name _____ Date _____

Latin American Revolutions

Read each question and its answer choices. Fill in the bubble in front of the word or words that best answer each question.

Questions marked with an asterisk (*) have more than one correct answer. For these questions, fill in the bubble next to *all* correct answers.

1. Which Latin American nation became the first black republic?
   - (a) Cuba
   - ⬤ Haiti
   - (c) Panama
   - (d) Colombia

2. One European country had colonies in most of South America. Which country was it?
   - (a) England
   - ⬤ Spain
   - (c) Portugal
   - (d) France

3. Which of the following best describes how Spain ruled its South American colonies?
   - (a) Spain selected Creoles to govern the colonies.
   - (b) Spain allowed most decisions to be made by the colonists.
   - ⬤ Spain kept tight control over the colonies.
   - (d) Spain shared control equally with the colonists.

---

4. "I was a slave on the French colony of Saint Domingue. I led a revolution and helped found the new nation of Haiti. Who am I?"
   - (a) Miguel Hidalgo
   - (b) Bernardo O'Higgins
   - ⬤ Toussaint L'Ouverture
   - (d) Francisco Miranda

5. A person from which of the following groups could rule a Spanish colony in South America?
   - (a) Indians
   - (b) mestizos
   - (c) Creoles
   - ⬤ Spaniards

6. Latin America includes _____.
   - (a) all of North America and part of South America
   - (b) all of Central America and all of North America
   - ⬤ part of North America, and all of Central and South America
   - (d) part of Central America, and all of North and South America

7. "I was a great South American revolutionary and general. I led military campaigns to free much of Spanish America. I was known as 'the Liberator.' Who am I?"
   - ⬤ Simón Bolívar
   - (b) Miquel Hidalgo
   - (c) Francisco Miranda
   - (d) José de San Martín

---

8. Democratic revolutions in which countries inspired many colonists in Spanish America to seek independence. Which two countries?
   - (a) France and Holland
   - ⬤ United States and France
   - (c) Spain and Portugal
   - (d) England and Scotland

9. "I was a Mexican priest. I gave a speech urging my people to rebel against Spain. I am known as the Father of Mexican Independence. Who am I?"
   - ⬤ Miguel Hidalgo
   - (b) José de San Martín
   - (c) Simón Bolívar
   - (d) Toussaint L'Ouverture

10. There were Creoles, mestizos, Indians, slaves, and Spaniards in South America. Those groups show that Spanish American colonies had _____.
    - (a) a new way of organizing government
    - ⬤ a strong class system based on birth
    - (c) settlers from many parts of Europe
    - (d) a large number of people making decisions

---

11. What did Creoles think about Spanish rule?
    - (a) They admired Spanish rule and were happy not to have the task of governing themselves.
    - ⬤ They resented Spanish control and wanted colonists to make more decisions.
    - (c) They were proud to be Spanish and pleased with their heritage of liberty.
    - (d) They were angry that Spaniards gave too much power to mestizos.

*12. Latin America was originally colonized by which of the following countries? (Select *all* that are correct.)
    - (a) Germany
    - ⬤ France
    - ⬤ Spain
    - ⬤ Portugal
    - (e) Italy

Latin American Revolutions

Scoring the Map Question: 13.

Count two points for each country correctly labeled. (Do not count points for the Extra

Challenge items, Chile and Argentina, which are based on material covered in an

optional lesson.)

Learning Coach Guide
Lesson 1: James Hargreaves and the Spinning Jenny

In the late eighteenth century, Great Britain led an Industrial Revolution that dramatically increased production of goods. The Industrial Revolution changed the way people worked and lived. Advances in the textile industry sparked this revolution. James Hargreaves's spinning jenny would make Britain a leader in cloth production.

Lesson Objectives

- Describe the Industrial Revolution as a time when more and more goods were produced by power-driven machinery.
- Explain that the Industrial Revolution began in England.
- Explain that during the Industrial Revolution production moved out of the home and into factories.
- Name some improvements in transportation that took place during the Industrial Revolution.
- Explain that in the early stages of the Industrial Revolution working conditions were harsh and workers suffered.
- Identify important figures, inventions, and ideas of the Industrial Revolution (James Watt, Robert Fulton, Charles Dickens, Karl Marx, spinning jenny, steam engine, steamboat, railroads, capitalism, Marxism).
- Explain that the Industrial Revolution was a change in the way people lived and produced things, and that it started in Great Britain.
- Recognize that many of the first innovations of the Industrial Revolution were in the textile industry.
- Identify James Hargreaves as the inventor of the spinning jenny.
- Describe the spinning jenny as a machine that spun many threads together and greatly increased the amount of thread available for weaving.
- Review important geographic knowledge and skills.

PREPARE

Approximate lesson time is 60 minutes.

Materials

> For the Student
>> Understanding Geography: Map Skills and Our World (Level 4)

Lesson Notes

James Hargreaves (c. 1720-1778) patented the spinning jenny in 1770, but probably invented it in 1764. The story told here recounts the traditional legend of Hargreaves's invention, which says that he got his idea when he saw his daughter overturn a spinning wheel. Some historians maintain that Hargreaves named the spinning jenny in honor of his daughter. Others believe that "jenny" came from "gin," which was short for "engine" (just as the "gin" in Eli Whitney's cotton gin was short for "engine").

You will need cotton balls if you choose to do the Beyond the Lesson activity. If necessary, you may substitute prepackaged cotton balls and skip the first two steps of the instructions.

Keywords and Pronunciation

loom : A frame or machine that weavers use to weave thread into cloth.

spindle : A round stick used to make thread while spinning.

spinning wheel : A machine for spinning thread.

TEACH

Activity 1: The Beginning of the Industrial Revolution (Online)

Instructions

This main teaching activity is online. Your student may complete this activity alone or with your help.

Activity 2: History Journal (Online)

Instructions

Read the History Journal entry for today's lesson. The following sample paragraph shows the main ideas for the topic of life before and after the Industrial Revolution. Compare your student's paragraph with the one below.

Life changed for most people after the Industrial Revolution. Before the Industrial Revolution, most people lived on farms. They worked in the fields with plows pulled by animals. They used horses and mules to get around. People spun their own thread by hand. They wove their own cloth and made their own clothes. Most people worked at home. After the Industrial Revolution, more people lived in the cities. More people worked in factories. People made cloth and thread with machines. They even plowed the land with machines. People could buy lots of different things in stores in the cities. The Industrial Revolution has changed the way we live today.

Activity 3: Presenting the James Hargreaves Exhibit (Online)

Instructions

The student will write a short oral presentation for a museum exhibit on James Hargreaves and the spinning jenny.

Activity 4: Geography Review (Online)

Instructions

It's time to look back and review some of the geography skills your student has learned before he takes the Geography Assessment in the next lesson. Have your student:

- Begin reviewing by clicking the online Geography Review.
- When he has finished the online review, have him go back to the Skill Builders in *Understanding Geography* Activities 1-12 and answer one question from each activity.
- If he has time, he may wish to answer the Map Review questions on pages 60–61 of *Understanding Geography*. They are optional.

Answers
Optional Map Review

1. See the map on page 60 to locate North America, South America, Europe, Africa, Asia, Australia, Antarctica, Pacific Ocean, Atlantic Ocean, Indian Ocean, and Artctic Ocean.
2. See the map on page 60.
3. Northern Hemisphere, Southern Hemisphere, Western Hemisphere, Eastern Hemisphere
4. Northern and Western Hemispheres
5. Latitude lines run east to west.
6. Asia
7. South America
8. Anchorage
9. 30°N, 90°W
10. You would travel northeast
11. Olympia
12. Mount Rainier
13. Spokane
14. 100 miles (160 kilometers)
15. Everett
16. Spokane
17. Cascade Range
18. Columbia River
19. northwest
20. Yakima, Walla Walla

ASSESS

Lesson Assessment: James Hargreaves and the Spinning Jenny (*Online*)

Students will complete an online assessment based on the lesson objectives. The assessment will be scored by the computer. The attached answer key is the most current and may not coincide with previously printed guides.

TEACH

Activity 5. Optional: James Hargreaves and the Spinning Jenny (*Online*)

Instructions

In this optional, offline activity, the student will spin thread from cotton by hand.

Learning Coach Guide
Lesson 2: James Watt and the Steam Engine

The Industrial Revolution got a huge boost when steam, instead of muscle, became a major source of power. James Watt made big improvements on earlier designs. His efficient steam engine made it possible to develop factories with power-driven machinery.

Lesson Objectives

- Explain that before the Industrial Revolution, people relied on animals, water, and their own muscles for power.
- Describe steam engines as important in the Industrial Revolution because they supplied much more power.
- Identify James Watt as a Scottish engineer who designed an efficient steam engine.
- Recognize that Watt's steam engine could be used to power many machines.
- Demonstrate mastery of important geographic knowledge and skills.

PREPARE

Approximate lesson time is 60 minutes.

Materials
For the Student
paper, 8 1/2" x 11"
pencils, colored, 16 colors or more

Keywords and Pronunciation
Erasmus Darwin (ih-RAZ-muhs DAHR-wuhn)
lunatic : A crazy person.

TEACH
Activity 1: A Full Head of Steam *(Online)*

Activity 2: History Journal *(Offline)*
Instructions
This activity requires the student to complete a paragraph with missing words. With your student, read the History Journal entry for today's lesson and compare it with the paragraph below. Did it include the most important parts of the lesson?
You will use the History Journal to assess the student's understanding of this lesson.

Before the Industrial Revolution took place, people had to use water, animals, or their own strength to run machines. Then James Watt, a Scottish engineer, invented a new and efficient steam engine. It did not use too much fuel. The steam engine was important because it could supply a lot of power. This invention could be used to run boats, trains, looms, and other machines.

Activity 3: Buy a Steam Engine! *(Offline)*
Instructions
Your student will plan and create an advertisement for James Watt's remarkable invention. You may want to use magazines, newspapers, or other sources for a model.

Activity 4. Optional: James Watt and the Steam Engine *(Online)*
Instructions
This website has detailed diagrams, a working steam engine, and some written explanations. You will need to participate in this activity with your student.

ASSESS

Lesson Assessment: James Watt and the Steam Engine, Part 1 *(Online)*
Students will complete an online assessment based on the lesson objectives. The assessment will be scored by the computer. The attached answer key is the most current and may not coincide with previously printed guides.

Lesson Assessment: James Watt and the Steam Engine, Part 2 *(Offline)*
Students will complete an offline assessment based on the lesson objectives. Print the assessment and have students complete it on their own. Use the answer key to score the assessment, and then enter the results online. The attached answer key is the most current and may not coincide with previously printed guides.

Lesson Assessment Answer Key

James Watt and the Steam Engine, Part 2

Answers:

1. Before the <u>Industrial Revolution</u> took place, people had to use <u>water</u>, <u>animals</u>, or their own strength to run <u>machines</u>. Then <u>James Watt</u>, a Scottish engineer, invented a new and efficient <u>steam engine</u>. It did not use too much fuel. The <u>steam engine</u> was important because it could supply a lot of <u>power</u>. This invention could be used to run boats, trains, looms, and other <u>machines</u>.

   Use the Grading Rubric below to award points for this question:

Did your student fill in the first blank with "<u>Industrial Revolution</u>"?	10 points
Did your student respond that people used "<u>water</u>", "<u>animals</u>" or their own strength to run "<u>machines</u>"?	10 points
Did your student identify "<u>James Watt</u>" and the Scottish engineer who invented a new and efficient "<u>steam engine</u>"?	10 points
Did your student respond that the "<u>steam engine</u>" was important because it could supply a lot of "<u>power</u>"?	10 points
Did your student respond that people used this invention to run boats, trains, looms and many other "<u>machines</u>"?	10 points

2. **Using the criteria listed below, enter the number of points your student earned based on the number of correctly labeled items.**

Did your student identify and label 10 - 11 items correctly?	50 pts.
Did your student identify and label 7 - 9 items correctly?	40 pts.
Did your student identify and label 4 - 6 items correctly?	25 pts.
Did your student identify and label 2 - 3 items correctly?	10 pts.
Did your student identify and label 1 item correctly?	5 pts.
Was your student unable to identify and label a single item correctly?	0 pts.

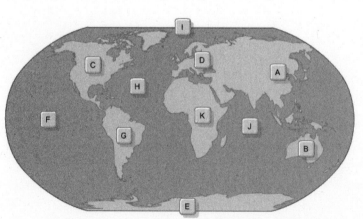

A. Asia

B. Australia

C. North America

D. Europe

E. Antarctica

F. Pacific Ocean

G. South America

H. Atlantic Ocean

I. Arctic Ocean

J. Indian Ocean

K. Africa

Learning Coach Guide
Lesson 3: Fulton and McAdam: A Revolution in Transportation

With the invention of the steam engine, the Industrial Revolution sped forward. Building on Watt's work, American inventor Robert Fulton made the first commercially successful steamboat. The steamboat spurred the building of canals on both sides of the Atlantic. In Britain, John Loudon McAdam worked on improving roads. His macadam pavement made travel by land faster, easier, and more efficient.

Lesson Objectives

- List the steamboat and better roads as major improvements in transportation.
- Identify Robert Fulton as the inventor of the first practical steamboat.
- Identify John McAdam as a man who improved the paving of roads.

PREPARE

Approximate lesson time is 60 minutes.

Keywords and Pronunciation

macadamized (muh-KA-duh-miyzd)

TEACH
Activity 1: Many Roads to Travel (Online)

Instructions

This main teaching activity is online. Your student may complete this activity alone or with your help.

Activity 2: History Journal (Offline)

Instructions

With your student, read the History Journal entry for today's lesson and compare it with the sample paragraph. Did it include the most important parts of the lesson?

People needed better transportation during the Industrial Revolution. Robert Fulton invented a good steamboat. Steamboats could go up and down rivers much faster than sailboats. John McAdam found a way to make better roads. He built them so that water would drain away. He also used small crushed stones. They made the roads smoother and harder. Now people could get around faster by water and by land.

Activity 3: Your Choice of Transportation? (Online)

Instructions

The student will write a short speech nominating either Robert Fulton or John McAdam for an imaginary award. The award recognizes the inventor's special progress in the field of transportation. This activity may require additional research online or in the library.

ASSESS

Lesson Assessment: Fulton and McAdam: A Revolution in Transportation
(*Online*)

Students will complete an offline assessment based on the lesson objectives. Print the assessment and have students complete it on their own. Use the answer key to score the assessment, and then enter the results online. The attached answer key is the most current and may not coincide with previously printed guides.

TEACH

Activity 4. Optional: Fulton and McAdam: A Revolution in Transportation *(Online)*
Instructions

Your student can learn more about Robert Fulton's steamship and John McAdam's roads by visiting the *Industrial Revolution* website.

Lesson Assessment Answer Key

Fulton and McAdam: A Revolution in Transportation

Answers:

1. the steamboat and better roads
2. Robert Fulton
3. John McAdam

Learning Coach Guide
Lesson 4: Americans Climb Aboard

The Industrial Revolution included a revolution in transportation. It sped up when locomotives began to use steam engines. Soon railroads became a speedy way to travel. Americans were among the first to develop the railroad.

Lesson Objectives
- Explain that the Industrial Revolution included a revolution in transportation.
- Explain that the steam-powered locomotive made it possible to move people and goods quickly over great distances.
- Explain that Americans used the railroad to connect the country from the Atlantic to the Pacific Ocean.

PREPARE

Approximate lesson time is 60 minutes.

Materials
For the Student

Inventors: A Library of Congress Book by Martin Sandler

map, U.S.

From Sea to Shining Sea activity sheet

Building the Transcontinental Railroad by Monica Halpern

TEACH
Activity 1: All Aboard: America Rides the Rails (Online)
Instructions
This main teaching activity begins online and concludes offline with a book. Your student may complete this activity alone or with your help.

Activity 2: History Journal (Offline)
Instructions
With your student, read the History Journal entry for today's lesson and compare it with the sample paragraph below. Did it include the most important parts of the lesson?

The railroads were an important part of the Industrial Revolution. Railroads started in England. That's where inventors put steam engines onto wagons. They used steam engines instead of horses to pull wagons over rails. Americans built lots of railroads. They lay thousands of miles of track. Before long they had half the railroad tracks in the world. They build a railroad that went from the Atlantic Ocean to the Pacific Ocean. The railroads changed the way that people lived. They made it easy to move people and goods a long way. The railroads brought a revolution in transportation.

Activity 3: From Sea to Shining Sea *(Offline)*
Instructions
The student will complete an activity sheet that reinforces the objectives for today's lesson. You will use the From Sea to Shining Sea activity sheet to assess your student's understanding of this lesson.
The answers to questions 1-3 are provided in the assessment section of this lesson.

Answers to Questions 4-10:
4. About 625 miles of track were laid between Sacramento and Ogden City.
5. It would have taken about 26 hours to travel from Omaha to Ogden City.
6. According to the scenario described, the distance between St. Louis and Chicago is about 240 miles.
7. The train would have been traveling 43.75 miles per hour.
8. It would have taken the team 35 days to lay track from Omaha to Kansas City.
9. The distance between New York and Sacramento is 2,775 miles.
10. It would have taken about three days to travel from Chicago to St. Louis by stagecoach.
Answer to Student Instructions Question:
[1] The transcontinental railway was completed.

Activity 4. Optional: Americans Climb Aboard *(Online)*
Instructions
In this offline optional activity, the student will read *Building the Transcontinental Railroad*, by Monica Halpern (Washington: National Geographic, 2002).

ASSESS
Lesson Assessment: Americans Climb Aboard (*Online*)
Review your student's responses on the Sea to Shining Sea Activity Sheet, and input the results online. The attached answer key is the most current and may not coincide with previously printed guides.

Lesson Assessment Answer Key

Americans Climb Aboard

Answers:

1. possible answers: transportation; the way people traveled
2. possible answers: the steam-powered locomotive; locomotives; railroads; trains
3. possible answers: railroad; transcontinental railroad; trains

Learning Coach Guide
Lesson 5: The First Factories

With the development of power-driven looms and large machinery, production moved out of homes and artisans' shops and into factories. The first factories, often dark and dangerous, forced huge changes in the rhythm of people's lives.

Lesson Objectives

- Explain that until the Industrial Revolution, most production of goods took place in homes and cottages.
- Explain that during the Industrial Revolution, power machinery was used in factories to produce many goods.
- Recognize that the first factories were textile mills.
- List two characteristics of early factory life (long regular hours, repetitive work, poor lighting, dangerous working conditions, child labor).

PREPARE

Approximate lesson time is 60 minutes.

Materials

For the Student

Lyddie by Katherine Paterson

Keywords and Pronunciation

piecer : A mill worker who put pieces of broken thread back together.

scavenger : A mill worker who picked up bits of fallen cotton.

TEACH
Activity 1: The Hard Life of Factory Workers (Online)

Instructions

This main teaching activity is online. Your student may complete this activity alone or with your help.

Activity 2: History Journal (Offline)

Instructions

With your student, read the History Journal entry for today's lesson and compare it with the sample paragraph below. Did it include the most important parts of the lesson?

Before the Industrial Revolution, people who made cloth worked in their cottages. Then big machines with steam engines came along. People needed to work in mills. The mills were very noisy places. There were lots of machines inside. Men, women, and children worked there. They worked long hours. They did not make much money. They had to do the same thing over and over again. The move from working at home to working in factories changed many people's lives.

Activity 3: Sarah's Neighbor Speaks to Parliament *(Offline)*

Instructions

The student will write and give a short speech to Parliament about the working conditions in English factories.

ASSESS

Lesson Assessment: The First Factories (*Online*)

Students will complete an online assessment based on the lesson objectives. The assessment will be scored by the computer. The attached answer key is the most current and may not coincide with previously printed guides.

TEACH

Activity 4. Optional: The First Factories *(Online)*

Instructions

In this optional offline activity, the student will read *Lyddie*, by Katherine Paterson (New York: Puffin, 1994). This historical fiction tells the story of a young Vermont farm girl who goes to work in a textile mill in Lowell, Massachusetts.

Learning Coach Guide
Lesson 6: Capitalism and New Wealth

Capitalism made the Industrial Revolution possible. Back in 1776, Adam Smith said nations would be wealthier if their governments stepped aside and let individuals make their own decisions about how to invest their money, or *capital*. That system spurred the Industrial Revolution.

Lesson Objectives

- Define *economy* as the way goods and services are produced and distributed.
- Name capitalism as a system in which individuals and private companies make decisions about the economy.
- Identify Adam Smith as a philosopher who wrote about capitalism.
- Name Great Britain's economy as the first capitalist economy.

PREPARE

Approximate lesson time is 60 minutes.

Materials

For the Student

📖 Let the People Decide

Keywords and Pronunciation

capitalism : A system in which individuals and companies make decisions about the economy.

economics : The study of how economies work.

economy : The way goods and services are produced and distributed.

TEACH
Activity 1: Adam Smith Has a Capital Idea *(Online)*
Instructions

This main teaching is online. Your student may complete this activity alone or with your help.

Activity 2: History Journal *(Offline)*
Instructions

With your student, read the History Journal entry for today's lesson and compare it with the sample paragraph below. Did it include the most important parts of the lesson?

Great Britain became a great trading nation because of capitalism. Capitalism means that people and companies decide what they want to sell. They make decisions about business. The government doesn't. Adam Smith wrote about capitalism in a book in 1776. He said it would make the economy strong. The economy is the way we make and sell things. People used capitalism in Great Britain to build factories and trade many things. Many countries use this system today.

Activity 3: Let the People Decide (Offline)
Instructions
Help your student complete the Let the People Decide activity sheet.

Answers:
1. Shields supplied consumers with clothes, tools, and sugar.
2. Shields was buying clothes and tools in England and shipping them to the West Indies, where he traded them for sugar. He would then have the sugar shipped to England, where he would sell it to consumers.
3. The consumers for the sugar were people in England. The consumers for the clothes and tools were people in the West Indies.
4. Answers should include two producers from the story. These producers include James Shields, who provided a trading service; a shipping company, which Shields paid to transport goods to the West Indies and sugar to England; plantation owners, who grew the sugar cane that was turned into sugar; textile mill owners and workers, who produced the cloth that was made into clothes that Shields traded for sugar; and tool makers, who produced the tools that Shields traded for sugar.
5. People in England liked sweets; they wanted it for their tea. Today, people like sugar in candy, cereal, coffee, and other foods.
6. Possible answers might include: There were no factories there to make clothes. People in the West Indies needed tools to work on the sugar plantations.
7. He probably would not have been successful. There would have been little demand for sugar in the West Indies. People there already had plenty of sugar since they were producing it.
8. The company's profit would be $80.00.
9. The company would have suffered losses. The losses would have been $20.00.

ASSESS

Lesson Assessment: Capitalism and New Wealth (Online)
Students will complete an online assessment based on the lesson objectives. The assessment will be scored by the computer. The attached answer key is the most current and may not coincide with previously printed guides.

Learning Coach Guide
Lesson 7. Optional: Charles Dickens: From Boy to Author

The great English writer Charles Dickens started life as a boy from a well-educated but struggling family. His father went to debtors' prison, and young Charles worked in a factory and experienced the life of the poor. Later he would write about it.

Lesson Objectives

- Identify Charles Dickens as a great author of the nineteenth century.
- Explain that as a boy Charles Dickens worked in a factory and experienced the life of the poor.
- Name two of Charles Dickens's famous works.

PREPARE

Approximate lesson time is 60 minutes.

Materials

> For the Student
>> History Journal
>> 🖳 Counting Centuries

Keywords and Pronunciation

debtors' prison : A prison for people who could not pay their debts.

TEACH
Activity 1. Optional: Optional Lesson Instructions (Online)
Instructions

This lesson is OPTIONAL. It is provided for students who seek enrichment or extra practice. You may skip this lesson.

If you choose to skip this lesson, then go to the Plan or Lesson Lists page and mark this lesson "Skipped" in order to proceed to the next lesson in the course.

Activity 2. Optional: A Dickens of a Time (Online)
Instructions

Activity 3. Optional: History Journal (Offline)

Instructions

With your student, read the History Journal entry for today's lesson and compare it with the sample paragraph below. Did it include the most important parts of the lesson?

You will use the History Journal to assess the student's understanding of this lesson.

Charles Dickens was a great writer. He lived in England during the Industrial Revolution. His father had problems spending too much money, so his family became poor. Charles's father had to go to debtors' prison. Charles had to work in a factory. He was lonely and unhappy there. He started to write stories about the people he saw. One of his stories was printed in a magazine. That's how Charles Dickens became a writer.

The paragraph should include answers to the following questions:
1. Who was Charles Dickens?
   Charles Dickens was a great author of the nineteenth century.
2. How did Dickens know about the lives of poor factory workers?
   As a boy, Charles Dickens worked in a factory and experienced the life of the poor.
3. What country, in what period in history, did most of Dickens's work deal with?
   His writing dealt with people in England during the Industrial Revolution.

Activity 4. Optional: Counting Centuries (Offline)
Instructions
The student will complete an activity sheet that explains the concept of centuries.

Answers:
1. eighteenth
2. the seventeenth century
3. nineteenth
4. 18
5. the twentieth century

Activity 5. Optional: Charles Dickens: From Boy to Author (Offline)
Instructions
Charles Dickens's novels are beyond the reading level of most fourth graders. However, some of his works have been adapted for young readers. You may wish to see if your local library has any such books. Many of his works have also been made into movies, which can help children get a flavor of Dickens's themes and characters. These two musicals are examples:

Scrooge (based on *A Christmas Carol*), 1970, Twentieth Century Fox (86 minutes, rated G)

Oliver! (based on *Oliver Twist*), 1968, Columbia/Tristar Pictures (145 minutes, rated G)

Learning Coach Guide
Lesson 8. Optional: Charles Dickens, the Author

Charles Dickens's vivid writing captured the hearts of Englishmen. He held a mirror up to a nation. He wrote things that made people laugh, but he also wrote about the hard life of the poor and abandoned in Industrial England.

Lesson Objectives
- Describe working and living conditions for the urban poor in Dickens's time.
- Explain that Charles Dickens used his writing to move people to try to solve the problems of the cities and make life better for the workers.

PREPARE

Approximate lesson time is 60 minutes.

Materials
> For the Student
>> History Journal
>> 📖 From A Christmas Carol by Charles Dickens

TEACH
Activity 1. Optional: Optional Lesson Instructions (Online)
Instructions
This lesson is OPTIONAL. It is provided for students who seek enrichment or extra practice. You may skip this lesson.

If you choose to skip this lesson, then go to the Plan or Lesson Lists page and mark this lesson "Skipped" in order to proceed to the next lesson in the course.

Activity 2. Optional: The Very Dickens (Online)

Activity 3. Optional: History Journal (Offline)
Instructions
With your student, read the History Journal entry for today's lesson and compare it with the sample paragraph below. Did it include the most important parts of the lesson? Did he identify at least two of Dickens's famous works?

Charles Dickens became a famous writer. His books made people laugh and cry. They made people think about how poor people had hard lives. Dickens visited America, but he did not have a very good time there. He grew very rich and bought the house that his father had shown him when he was a boy. He read his books to people on stage to make more money. He worked so hard he got sick, though. Charles Dickens died, but his books are still famous. They include *The Pickwick Papers, Oliver Twist, A Christmas Carol, Great Expectations,* and *A Tale of Two Cities.*

Activity 4. Optional: Charles Dickens, the Author *(Offline)*
Instructions
Let your student find an interesting passage from one of Dickens's books and give a dramatic reading of it in front of an audience.

Your student may also print the selection from *A Christmas Carol.*

Learning Coach Guide
Lesson 9: Karl Marx in London

Karl Marx wrote about how he imagined the end of the class struggle. He said that one day the working classes would rise up and revolt against the owners of industry. In the end, Marx thought the government would own everything. And he thought it would distribute wealth wisely.

Lesson Objectives

- Explain that during the Industrial Revolution there were large differences in the way the rich and poor lived.
- Describe Karl Marx as a philosopher and revolutionary.
- Explain that Marx predicted a revolution in which the working classes would rise up and overthrow the owners of industry.
- Recognize that the terms *Marxism* and *communism* refer to the work and theories of Karl Marx.

PREPARE

Approximate lesson time is 60 minutes.

Lesson Notes

This lesson presents a brief, simple introduction to the thought of Karl Marx (1818-1883). It is intended to introduce a major figure and his ideas, helping students understand some of the thinking that would fuel the Russian Revolution and frame major political divisions of the twentieth century. This lesson is not intended to deal with the complexity and range of Marx's work. Marx regarded capitalism as the most efficient and dynamic economic system yet devised, but considered its distribution of wealth its greatest flaw. He predicted a revolution between the proletariat (working class) and bourgeoisie (owners of the means of production) that would end in the elimination of private ownership. In this lesson we have substituted the term "working class" for "proletariat," and the term "owners of industry" or "new middle class" for "bourgeoisie."

TEACH
Activity 1: Karl Marx and Communism *(Online)*

Instructions

This main teaching activity is online. Your student may complete this activity alone or with your help.

Activity 2: History Journal *(Offline)*

Instructions

With your student, read the History Journal entry for today's lesson and compare it with the sample paragraph below. Did it include the most important parts of the lesson?

Karl Marx lived in London. He was a philosopher. He was also a revolutionary. Marx didn't like the way the poor people had to live during Industrial Revolution. The poor people did not make much money. They had hard lives. Marx didn't think that was fair. He thought that a revolution was coming. He thought the workers would rise up and take away the factories from the owners. Then everyone would work together. Marx called this *communism.*

Activity 3: An Interview with Karl Marx *(Offline)*
Instructions
In this offline activity, the student will write questions for an interview with Karl Marx.

ASSESS
Lesson Assessment: Karl Marx in London (*Online*)
Students will complete an online assessment based on the lesson objectives. The assessment will be scored by the computer. The attached answer key is the most current and may not coincide with previously printed guides.

Learning Coach Guide
Lesson 10: The Great Exhibition

Known as "the workshop of the world," Great Britain leapt into the lead of the Industrial Revolution. In 1851, the nation displayed its wealth and abilities at the Great Exhibition. This giant fair in London showed what the Industrial Revolution had made possible.

You will evaluate the poster your student creates for the Come to the Great Exhibition! activity and use it as the assessment for this lesson.

Lesson Objectives

- Explain that Britain had become the world's leader in the Industrial Revolution.
- Name Victoria as the British queen who reigned during this period.
- Describe the Great Exhibition as a fair that displayed British goods, abilities, and successes.
- Recognize that Britain was known as "the workshop of the world" and that the British had a strong sense of pride in their nation.

PREPARE

Approximate lesson time is 60 minutes.

Keywords and Pronunciation
Koh-i-noor (KOH-uh-noor)

TEACH
Activity 1: England and Miracles of Modern Industry (Online)

Instructions

This main teaching activity is online. Your student may complete this activity alone or with your help.

Activity 2: Come to the Great Exhibition! (Offline)

Instructions

In this offline activity, your student will create a poster that advertises the Great Exhibition. You will evaluate this project and use it as the lesson assessment.

ASSESS

Lesson Assessment: The Great Exhibition (*Online*)

Review your student's responses on the Come to the Great Exhibition! activity and input the results online. The attached answer key is the most current and may not coincide with previously printed guides.

TEACH
Activity 3. Optional: The Great Exhibition *(Online)*
Instructions

In this optional online activity, the student will visit two websites to learn about some other international fairs and expositions that came after the Great Exhibition.

TEACH

Lesson Assessment Answer Key

The Great Exhibition

Answers:

Answers will vary. Use the Grading Rubric below to award points for this question:

Did your student include, in some way, the fact that Britain had become the world's leader in the Industrial Revolution?	10 pts.
Did your student include, in some way, the fact that Victoria was the British queen who reigned when the Great Exhibition was held?	10 pts.
Did your student include, in some way, the fact that the Great Exhibition was a fair that displayed British goods, abilities, and successes?	10 pts.
Did your student include, in some way, the fact that Britain was known as "the workshop of the world"?	10 pts.
Did your student include, in some way, the fact that the British had a strong sense of pride in their nation?	10 pts.
Total:	

Learning Coach Guide
Lesson 11: Unit Review and Assessment

The student will review this unit and take the unit assessment.

Lesson Objectives

- Demonstrate mastery of important knowledge and skills in this unit.
- Recognize that many of the first innovations of the Industrial Revolution were in the textile industry.
- Identify James Hargreaves as the inventor of the spinning jenny.
- List the steamboat and better roads as major improvements in transportation.
- Identify Robert Fulton as the inventor of the first practical steamboat.
- Explain that the steam-powered locomotive made it possible to move people and goods quickly over great distances.
- Explain that Americans used the railroad to connect the country from the Atlantic to the Pacific Ocean.
- Explain that until the Industrial Revolution, most production of goods took place in homes and cottages.
- Explain that during the Industrial Revolution, power machinery was used in factories to produce many goods.
- List two characteristics of early factory life (long regular hours, repetitive work, poor lighting, dangerous working conditions, child labor).
- Name capitalism as a system in which individuals and private companies make decisions about the economy.
- Describe Karl Marx as a philosopher and revolutionary.
- Explain that Britain had become the world's leader in the Industrial Revolution.
- Name Victoria as the British queen who reigned during this period.
- Name Great Britain's economy as the first capitalist economy.
- Explain that before the Industrial Revolution, people relied on animals, water, and their own muscles for power.
- Describe steam engines as important in the Industrial Revolution because they supplied much more power.
- Identify James Watt as a Scottish engineer who designed an efficient steam engine.
- Describe the Industrial Revolution as a time when more and more goods were produced by power-driven machinery.
- Explain that the Industrial Revolution began in England.
- Explain that during the Industrial Revolution production moved out of the home and into factories.
- Explain that in the early stages of the Industrial Revolution working conditions were harsh and workers suffered.

PREPARE

Approximate lesson time is 60 minutes.

TEACH
Activity 1: The Industrial Revolution (Offline)
Instructions
The student will review this unit and take the unit assessment.

Answers:

[1] Great Britain

[2] James Hargreaves

[3] the spinning jenny

[4] the steam engine

[5] in homes and cottages

[6] Robert Fulton

[7] a way to pave roads so that they were smooth

[8] the United States

[9] Possible answer: Americans were trying to connect a continent that went from the Atlantic to the Pacific.

[10] capitalism

[11] Charles Dickens

[12] Charles's family had money when he was very young, but then they met with hard times. Charles had to work in factories as a child.

[13] Karl Marx

[14] Marxism

[15] Victoria

[16] all the products of the Industrial Revolution

Activity 2: History Journal Review (Offline)
Instructions
The student will use the History Journal to review for the unit assessment. You can help by asking questions based on the work in the journal.

Activity 3: Online Interactive Review (Online)
Instructions
The student will continue reviewing the unit by completing an online interactive review.

ASSESS

Unit Assessment: The Industrial Revolution (Offline)

Students will complete an offline Unit Assessment. Print the assessment and have students complete it on their own. Use the answer key to score the assessment, and then enter the results online. The attached answer key is the most current and may not coincide with previously printed guides.

The Industrial Revolution

Name _____ Date _____

The Industrial Revolution

Read each question and its answer choices. Fill in the bubble in front of
the word or words that best answer each question.

1. Many of the first innovations of the Industrial Revolution made
   England a leader in what industry?
   - ⓐ wine production
   - ⓑ shipbuilding
   - ● textile manufacture
   - ⓓ hotels

2. Why were steam engines important in the Industrial Revolution?
   - ● They provided a lot more power than people and
     animals could.
   - ⓑ They supplied electricity to homes and factories.
   - ⓒ They made it possible to build skyscrapers.
   - ⓓ They moved production from the factory to the home.

3. What was one big effect of the Industrial Revolution?
   - ● More and more goods were produced by powerful machines.
   - ⓑ More nations abandoned factories and steam engines.
   - ⓒ Farmland became available to English shepherds
     and peasants.
   - ⓓ A revolution of workers took place in England.

4. What made it possible to move people and goods quickly over great
   distances in the 1800s?
   - ⓐ stagecoaches
   - ● steam-powered locomotives
   - ⓒ prairie schooners
   - ⓓ airplanes

5. Before the Industrial Revolution, where did most production of
   goods take place?
   - ⓐ in factories
   - ● in homes and cottages
   - ⓒ in schools and monasteries
   - ⓓ in office buildings

6. In what economic system are individual people and private
   companies in charge of making economic choices?
   - ⓐ communism
   - ⓑ socialism
   - ● capitalism
   - ⓓ traditionalism

7. Which country had the world's first capitalist economy?
   - ⓐ France
   - ● Great Britain
   - ⓒ Germany
   - ⓓ Portugal

8. During the Industrial Revolution, Britain was known as "the
   workshop of the world." Why?
   - ● Britain was the leader of the Industrial Revolution.
   - ⓑ Most of the world's workers lived there.
   - ⓒ Britain produced more railroad track than any other country.
   - ⓓ All of the world's crystal was made there.

9. What philosopher living in London wrote about class struggle and
   against owners of industry?
   - ⓐ James Hargreaves
   - ⓑ Charles Dickens
   - ● Karl Marx
   - ⓓ Prince Albert

10. What country took the lead in building railroads?
    - ⓐ Germany
    - ⓑ Ireland
    - ● the United States
    - ⓓ France

11. During the early Industrial Revolution, what were working conditions
    like for factory workers?
    - ⓐ The factories were well lit and clean, but the hours were long.
    - ● The hours were long and the factories were dark and unsafe.
    - ⓒ Women and children worked few hours, but men worked
      long hours.
    - ⓓ The pay was good, and most people were quite happy.

12. Which of these were major improvements in transportation during
    the Industrial Revolution?
    - ⓐ highways and monorails
    - ⓑ submarines and airplanes
    - ⓒ sailing ships and hot air balloons
    - ● steamboats and better roads

Match the name of each person on the left with a description of the
person on the right. Write the letter of the description on the line in front of
the name. There is one extra description on the right that does not match
any of the names.

13. **D** James Hargreaves   A. Inventor of the first
                                   practical steamboat

    E James Watt   B. Queen of England during the
                                   Industrial Revolution

    A Robert Fulton   C. Improved the paving of roads

    B Victoria   D. Inventor of the spinning jenny

                               E. Designed an efficient steam
                                  engine

The Industrial Revolution

14. Write a paragraph about the Industrial Revolution. Include the following.

- Tell where the Industrial Revolution started.
- Explain how the production of goods changed.
- Explain what effect this had on where people lived.
- Describe what factory life was like.

A topic sentence is provided. Write neatly in complete sentences. Check your spelling, capitalization, and punctuation. End your paragraph with a concluding sentence.

Between 1750 and 1850, the Industrial Revolution changed the world. _____

_____
_____
_____
_____
_____
_____
_____
_____
_____
_____
_____
_____
_____

Scoring the Essay Question

This essay question is worth four points. Score the student's writing as follows:

- One point for stating that the Industrial Revolution started in Great Britain.

- One point for explaining the following points: Before the Industrial Revolution, the production of goods took place mostly in homes and cottages, using power supplied by animals, water, and people. After the Industrial Revolution started, production moved to factories and power was supplied by steam engines.

- One point for explaining that when production moved from homes and cottages to factories, people moved from farms (the country) to cities.

- One point if the student included at least two of the following characteristics in his description of factory life:

  Factory workers worked long hours.
  The work was repetitious (they did the same thing over and over).
  There was poor lighting in the factories.
  Working conditions were dangerous.
  Children, many very young, worked in the factories.

Learning Coach Guide
Lesson 1: A New Kind of Czar: Peter the Great

Russia's Peter the Great was very interested in the changes happening in western Europe during the Scientific Revolution and the start of the Industrial Revolution. He brought many western ways to Russia, despite resistance from some Russians.

Lesson Objectives

- Explain that many nations came into being and grew stronger at this time.
- Describe nationalism as a strong sense of pride in one's nation.
- Describe the growth of Russia, and name some major Russian leaders (Peter the Great, Catherine the Great, Nicholas II).
- Name Germany and Italy as two European nations that developed into single countries in the nineteenth century.
- State that the question of whether to allow slavery's expansion into the new American territories led to a bloody civil war won by the North.
- Identify key figures and events that promoted nationalism (Ypsilanti, Lincoln, U.S. Civil War, Brothers Grimm, Bismarck, Garibaldi).
- Explain that the first modern Olympics began in the late 1800s with the growth of nationalism.
- Locate Russia and the Ural Mountains on a map.
- Define *czar* as the Russian leader.
- Describe Peter the Great as a czar who tried to bring western ways to Russia.
- Name St. Petersburg as the city built by Peter the Great.

PREPARE

Approximate lesson time is 60 minutes.

Materials

For the Student

- 📖 Map of Europe, 1725
- 📖 Map of Russia, 1725-1855

Keywords and Pronunciation

czar (zahr) : The Russian ruler.

nationalism : a strong feeling of attachment to one´s own country

Okhotsk (uh-KAWTSK)

Urals (YOUR-uhls)

TEACH
Activity 1: A Great Country and Its Great Czar *(Online)*
Instructions
This main teaching activity is online. You may wish to help your student with the maps and the different scales they display.

Activity 2: History Journal *(Offline)*
Instructions
With your student, read the History Journal entry for today's lesson and compare it with the sample paragraph. Did it include the most important parts of the lesson?

Peter the Great was a czar who brought western ways to Russia. As the Russian leader, he thought that Russia needed to change. He liked some of the new ideas in western Europe. He traveled to England and other countries. He asked many questions. He learned how to build ships and do other things. Then he went back to Russia to make changes. He built a new city called St. Petersburg. He wanted it to look like the cities in Europe. Peter the Great did a lot to change his country.

Ask your student to point to Russia and the Ural Mountains on the map.

You will use the History Journal to assess the student's understanding of this lesson.

Activity 3: Peter the Great in Europe *(Online)*
Instructions
In this online activity, the student will identify where Peter the Great went and what he learned when he took his grand tour of Europe.

Activity 4. Optional: A New Kind of Czar: Peter the Great *(Online)*
Instructions
Your student may take a virtual tour of St. Petersburg or read *St. Petersburg* (Cities of the World Series) by Deborah Kent (New York: Children's Press, 1977).

As usual, preview the recommended book or website listed here before having your student view it.

ASSESS
Lesson Assessment: A New Kind of Czar: Peter the Great *(Online)*
Review your student's responses on the History Journal activity, and input the results online. The attached answer key is the most current and may not coincide with previously printed guides.

Lesson Assessment Answer Key

A New Kind of Czar: Peter the Great

Answers:

1. The Ural Mountains are between "Europe" and "Siberia" on the map.

2. Answers will vary. Use the grading rubric below to award points for this question.

Did your student include, in some way, the fact that the czar was the Russian leader?	10 points
Did your student include, in some way, the fact that as czar, Peter tried to bring western ways to Russia?	10 points
Did your student include, in some way, the fact that Peter the Great built a new city called St. Petersburg?	10 points
Total:	

Learning Coach Guide
Lesson 2: Catherine the Great

An ambitious German princess, Catherine the Great ruled Russia for more than three decades. She expanded Russia's borders. Like Peter the Great, Catherine was attracted to western ideas, but serfdom grew during her reign.

Lesson Objectives

- Explain that serfdom grew under Catherine the Great's reign.
- Explain that Catherine the Great expanded Russia to the Black Sea.
- Describe Catherine as attracted to western ideas.
- Identify Catherine the Great as an empress of Russia.

PREPARE

Approximate lesson time is 60 minutes.

Materials

For the Student

- 🖥 Map of Russia, 1725-1855
- 🖥 Sea Routes to Southern Russia activity sheet
- 🖥 Build a Potemkin Village Worksheet

Lesson Notes

Catherine the Great lived from 1729 to 1796.

Keywords and Pronunciation

ambassador : An official who goes to another country to represent his or her own country.

Crimea (kriy-MEE-uh)

czar (zahr) : The Russian ruler.

Dnieper (NEE-pur)

Grigory Potemkin (grih-GOR-ee poh-TEM-kin)

Kiev (KEE-ef)

TEACH
Activity 1: Russia Gets Another "Great" Leader (Online)
Instructions

This main teaching activity is online. Your student may want to complete this activity alone or with your help.

Activity 2: History Journal (Offline)
Instructions
With your student, read the History Journal entry for today's lesson and compare it with the sample paragraph below. Did it include the most important parts of the lesson?

Catherine the Great was a famous empress of Russia. Peter the Great wanted to bring western ways to Russia. So did Catherine the Great. She wanted to make Russia bigger. She conquered land along the Black Sea. That way Russian ships could trade. Catherine did not do much to help the serfs. They lived very hard lives.

Activity 3: The Crimea: Russia's Southern Trading Door (Offline)
Instructions
In this offline activity, your student will define and draw trade routes to and from Russia's Crimean Peninsula. Likely routes would go by sea from Crimea past Istanbul and through the Aegean Sea to the Mediterranean Sea. From there they could to Egypt, Italy, France, Spain, Morocco, England, and the Americas. The passages between the Black Sea and the Aegean Sea, and between Spain and Morocco are the best points on the map to control shipping because they are narrow.

Activity 4. Optional: Catherine the Great (Offline)
Instructions
Your student will build a Potemkin village from an activity sheet.

ASSESS
Lesson Assessment: Catherine the Great (Online)
Students will complete an offline assessment based on the lesson objectives. Print the assessment and have students complete it on their own. Use the answer key to score the assessment, and then enter the results online. The attached answer key is the most current and may not coincide with previously printed guides.

Lesson Assessment Answer Key

Catherine the Great

Answers:

1. Russia

2. True. Serfdom grew in Russia under Catherine's reign.

3. False. She was attracted to western ideas.

4. Catherine expanded Russia to the Black Sea.

Learning Coach Guide
Lesson 3: Nicholas Nixes Change

When Napoleon invaded Russia in 1812, the Russians pushed him back. But French revolutionary ideas spread with his march. When Czar Nicholas came to power, he made sure they didn't take hold in Russia.

Lesson Objectives
- Explain that ideas about liberty, revolutions, and constitutions spread to Russia.
- Describe Nicholas as a czar whose reign was harsh, and who was dedicated to stopping the spread of those ideas.
- State that Nicholas was known as "the policeman of Europe."

PREPARE

Approximate lesson time is 60 minutes.

Materials
For the Student
> History Journal
> > 📖 Policeman of Europe Activity Sheet

TEACH
Activity 1: Nicholas Says "No" to Change (Online)
Instructions
This main teaching activity is online. Your student may complete this activity alone or with your help.

Activity 2: History Journal (Offline)
Instructions
With your student, read the History Journal entry for today's lesson and compare it with the sample paragraph below. Did it include the most important parts of the lesson?

Nicholas I was a czar of Russia. He tried to stop ideas about revolutions and liberty. Some serfs and nobles in Russia wanted change. But Nicholas did not. He wanted to crush revolutions. He stopped them in Russia. He stopped them in Poland and Hungary. People called Nicholas the policeman of Europe.

Activity 3: Policeman of Europe *(Offline)*

Instructions

You will use this activity sheet to assess your student's understanding of today's lesson.

Answers to the questions on the Policeman of Europe activity sheet are :

1. Possible answers: ideas about liberty, republics, revolution, constitutions.

2. Policeman

3. Sample Answer: Nicholas thought that the ideas spreading into Russia were dangerous and bad for Russia. He decided to protect Russia from these ideas by crushing revolution and reform in and around Russia. His reign was harsh. He tried to control the Russian people's travel, education, speech, and writing.

ASSESS

Lesson Assessment: Nicholas Nixes Change (*Online*)

Review your student's responses on the *Policeman of Europe Activity Sheet*, and input the results online. The attached answer key is the most current and may not coincide with previously printed guides.

Lesson Assessment Answer Key

Nicholas Nixes Change

Answers:

1. Possible answers include: ideas about liberty, republics, constitutions and revolution.

2. Policeman

3. Sample Answer: Nicholas thought that the ideas spreading into Russia were dangerous and bad for Russia. He decided to protect Russia from these ideas by crushing revolution and reform in and around Russia. His reign was harsh. He tried to control the Russian people's travel, education, speech, and writing.

Learning Coach Guide
Lesson 4. Optional: Greece Against the Ottoman Empire

The vast Ottoman Empire ruled many different peoples. The Greeks united to throw off the Ottoman rulers. Greece, the historic home of democracy, became an independent nation in the 1820s.

Lesson Objectives

- Locate the Ottoman Empire, Greece, and the Balkan Peninsula on a map.
- Describe the Ottoman Empire as a vast Muslim empire.
- Explain that the Greeks fought for and won independence from the Ottoman Turks.
- Explain why the Greeks were so proud of their ancient heritage.

PREPARE

Approximate lesson time is 60 minutes.

Materials

For the Student

  🏛 Map of the Ottoman Empire, 1798-1920

  History Journal

  🏛 Greece: Then and Now

Lesson Notes

If your child did not study the K12 second and third grade history programs, which included introductions to Islam and to the great Muslim empires of the Middle Ages and the Renaissance, you may wish to review the following lessons:

Muhammad and the Beginning of Islam

Islam Becomes an Empire

Glories of Greece

The Rising Ottoman Turks

You must go to the Maps, Scales, and Finding Our Place lesson in Unit 1 to find the links to these lessons.

The Greek independence movement lasted from 1821 to 1832.

Keywords and Pronunciation

Alexander Ypsilanti (uhl-yik-SAHN-dur ip-sih-LAN-tee)

Istanbul (ihs-TAHN-bool)

TEACH
Activity 1. Optional: Optional Lesson Instructions *(Online)*

Instructions

This lesson is OPTIONAL. It is provided for students who seek enrichment or extra practice. You may skip this lesson.

If you choose to skip this lesson, then go to the Plan or Lesson Lists page and mark this lesson "Skipped" in order to proceed to the next lesson in the course.

Activity 2. Optional: The Ottomans' Unruly Empire *(Online)*
Instructions
This teaching activity is online. Your student may want to complete this activity by herself, or you may want to join her at the computer as she reads about the Greek fight for independence.

Activity 3. Optional: History Journal *(Offline)*
Instructions
With your student, read the History Journal entry for today's lesson and compare it with the sample paragraph below. Did it include the most important parts of the lesson?

The Ottoman Turks had a huge empire that included Greece and the rest of the Balkan Peninsula. The Greeks did not want to be ruled by the Ottoman Turks. The Greeks were proud of their history and wanted freedom. They fought for their independence. People from other countries finally helped the Greeks win their freedom from the Ottoman Turks.

Activity 4. Optional: Greece: Then and Now *(Offline)*
Instructions
Your student will use the Greece: Then and Now activity sheet to compare Greece under Ottoman rule with today's Greece.
Answers to page 1:
Balkan
Ottoman
Muslim
detested
poor
backward
Europe
proud
democracy

Learning Coach Guide
Lesson 5. Optional: The New American Nationalism

While Europeans recoiled from the revolution spearheaded by France and unleashed by Napoleon, a new spirit of democratic nationalism swept the United States. The Louisiana Purchase had opened new territories for exploration and settlement. By the 1820s American painters, writers, and poets began to celebrate the American experience.

Lesson Objectives

- Describe Americans as proud of their democracy.
- Explain that Americans were moving west and were enthusiastic about the frontier.
- Describe George Caleb Bingham as an important painter of early American life.
- Characterize Bingham's paintings as filled with admiration for the American landscape, democracy, and people.

PREPARE

Approximate lesson time is 60 minutes.

Materials
> For the Student
>> History Journal
>> paper, 8 1/2" x 11"
>> pencils, colored, 16 colors or more

TEACH
Activity 1. Optional: Optional Lesson Instructions (Online)
Instructions

This lesson is OPTIONAL. It is provided for students who seek enrichment or extra practice. You may skip this lesson.

If you choose to skip this lesson, then go to the Plan or Lesson Lists page and mark this lesson "Skipped" in order to proceed to the next lesson in the course.

Activity 2. Optional: George Caleb Bingham Celebrates America (Online)
Instructions

This main teaching activity is online. Your student may complete this activity alone or with your help.

Activity 3. Optional: History Journal *(Offline)*

Instructions

With your student, read the History Journal entry for today's lesson and compare it with the sample paragraph below. Did it include the most important parts of the lesson?

George Caleb Bingham was a famous American painter. He liked to paint pictures of Indians, farmers, and people on the frontier. He also liked to paint pictures about elections. He thought democracy was very important. Not everyone in America could vote. But people in Europe still had to live under kings and queens. People in America were free from kings and queens. Americans were proud of democracy. They loved their country.

Activity 4. Optional: A Banner for Democracy *(Online)*

Instructions

After taking a second look at three of Bingham's paintings, your student will create a banner that celebrates democracy.

Activity 5. Optional: The New American Nationalism *(Online)*

Instructions

In this optional online activity, the student will view Bingham's *Boatmen on the Missouri*.

Learning Coach Guide
Lesson 6: One Nation or Two?

Americans were enthusiastic about their nation's democracy and rapid westward expansion. But northern and southern sections of the country had developed in different ways. As the young United States expanded, North and South clashed about whether slavery be allowed to expand in a land where "all men are created equal."

Lesson Objectives
- Explain that the southern states depended on plantation agriculture and slave labor.
- Explain that the northern states depended mainly on small farms, growing industry, and free labor.
- Explain that the expansion of the United States raised the question of whether slavery should be allowed to expand.

PREPARE

Approximate lesson time is 60 minutes.

Materials
For the Student

History Journal

- Confederate and Union States, 1861
- Free State or Slave State Activity Sheet
- Map of Slavery in the U.S., 1850

The Bushwhacker: A Civil War Adventure by Jennifer Johnson Garrity

Keywords and Pronunciation
Dubuque (duh-BYOOK)

TEACH
Activity 1: A Divided Nation (Online)
Instructions
The main teaching activity is online. Your student may complete this activity alone or with your help.

Activity 2: History Journal (Offline)
Instructions
With your student, read the History Journal entry for today's lesson and compare it with the sample paragraph below. Did it include the most important parts of the lesson?

Joshua lived up North. His family did not own slaves. He took a trip to St. Louis to visit his grandfather. In St. Louis people had slaves. People in the South used slaves on farms and plantations. They wanted new states to be places where people could own slaves. People in the North didn't need slaves. They didn't think new states should have slaves. The question of slavery would not go away.

Activity 3: Free State or Slave State *(Online)*
Instructions
The student will complete a map-based activity sheet which will be used as the lesson assessment for today.

Activity 4: One Nation or Two? *(Offline)*
Instructions
In this optional activity, the student can read *The Bushwhacker: A Civil War Adventure,* by Jennifer Johnson Garrity (Atlanta: Peachtree Publishers, 1999).

ASSESS
Lesson Assessment: One Nation or Two? (*Online*)
Review your student's responses on the *Free State or Slave State* activity sheet, and input the results online. The attached answer key is the most current and may not coincide with previously printed guides.

Name _____   Date _____

Lesson Assessment Answer Key

One Nation or Two?

Answers:

1. plantation agriculture; slave labor
2. small farms; growing industry; free labor
3. slaves

Learning Coach Guide
Lesson 7: The Civil War Makes One Nation

Would the United States continue to exist as a single nation? Would slavery spread and continue? The Civil War answered those questions. It was America's bloodiest conflict, but it ended slavery and ensured that the United States would be one nation.

Lesson Objectives

- Describe the expansion of slavery into the new territories as the issue that divided North from South.
- Explain that after Abraham Lincoln was elected president, several southern states seceded from the Union.
- Describe the Civil War as America's bloodiest war.
- Describe the Civil War as the war that ended slavery and confirmed that the United States was a single nation.

PREPARE

Approximate lesson time is 60 minutes.

Materials

For the Student

History Journal

- ▣ Map of Confederate and Union States, 1861 (b/w)
- ▣ Map of Confederate and Union States, 1861 (color)
- ▣ Mapping the Civil War Activity Sheet

Keywords and Pronunciation

Manassas (muh-NA-suhs)

secede : To withdraw from an organization.

Ulysses (you-LIH-seez)

TEACH
Activity 1: One Nation (Online)

Instructions

This main teaching activity is online. Your student may complete this activity alone or with your help as she reads how the civl war makes one nation.

Activity 2: History Journal *(Offline)*
Instructions
With your student, read the History Journal entry for today's lesson and compare it with the sample paragraph below. Did it include the most important parts of the lesson?

The North and the South did not stop arguing over slavery. When Abraham Lincoln was elected president, the states in the South decided to secede. They formed their own country. It was called the Confederate States of America. That started four years of war. It was the bloodiest war in American history. Americans fought each other. The North finally won. That meant no more slaves. It meant that all the states were one country again.

Activity 3: Mapping the Civil War *(Online)*
Instructions
The student will complete an offline mapping activity.
Answers to Questions 5-8
5. The issue that divided North from South was the expansion of slavery into the new territories.
6. After Abraham Lincoln was elected president, several southern states seceded from the Union.
7. The three-word phrase that best describes the Civil War is "America's bloodiest war."
8. The Civil War ended slavery and confirmed that the United States was a single nation.

Activity 4. Optional: The Civil War Makes One Nation *(Online)*
Instructions
In this optional online activity, the student will compare casualty figures from the Civil War with other wars the United States has been involved in.

ASSESS
Lesson Assessment: The Civil War Makes One Nation (*Online*)
Students will complete an offline assessment based on the lesson objectives. Print the assessment and have students complete it on their own. Use the answer key to score the assessment, and then enter the results online. The attached answer key is the most current and may not coincide with previously printed guides.

Name _____   Date _____

Lesson Assessment Answer Key

The Civil War Makes One Nation

Answers:

1. Possible answers: slavery; the expansion of slavery into the new territories.

2. Several southern states seceded from the Union.

3. Answers will vary but should somehow hint at the fact that it was America's bloodiest war.

4. Answer should include that the Civil War ended slavery.

5. The Civil War confirmed that the United States was a single nation.

Learning Coach Guide
Lesson 8: Lincoln's Leadership

Abraham Lincoln worked to make sure the United States of America remained one nation. He also helped Americans think about what their country stood for. He helped them understand that the terrible Civil War might result in "a new birth of freedom."

Lesson Objectives

- Identify Abraham Lincoln as president of the United States during the Civil War.
- Describe Lincoln as a man committed to saving the Union.
- Explain that Lincoln hoped the Civil War would bring about a "new birth of freedom" in the United States by ending slavery.
- Describe the Gettysburg Address as an important speech given by Lincoln during the Civil War.

PREPARE

Approximate lesson time is 60 minutes.

Materials

> For the Student
>> History Journal
>> 🖳 Gettysburg Address

Lesson Notes

Students who are strong readers may be able to read this entire lesson on their own. However, because this lesson includes the Gettysburg Address, most children will need adult assistance.

You may want to look up one or more of the following children's books on Lincoln and the Gettysburg address:
The Gettysburg Address by Abraham Lincoln, illustrated by Michael McCurdy (Boston: Houghton Mifflin, 1995)
Abraham Lincoln's Gettysburg Address: Four Score and More... by Barbara Silberdick Feinberg (Brookfield, CT: Twenty-First Century Books, 2000)
Just a Few Words, Mr. Lincoln: The Story of the Gettysburg Address by Jean Fritz, illustrated by Charles Robinson (New York: Grosset & Dunlap, 1993)

TEACH
Activity 1: Abraham Lincoln *(Online)*

Instructions

This main teaching activity is online. Your student may complete this activity alone or with your help.

Activity 2: Lincoln's Speechwriter (Offline)
Instructions
As a speechwriter for the president, the student must gather information for the Gettysburg Address. In her History Journal, she will write answers that Lincoln might have given to a series of questions.

Here are suggested answers for the questions:
1. Our ancestors gained their independence from Great Britain and created a new nation.
2. liberty and equality
3. whether our nation, or any democratic nation, can endure for long
4. to keep the country together
5. the soldiers who fought and died on this battleground
6. winning the war and preserving the Union
7. government of the people, by the people, for the people

ASSESS
Lesson Assessment: Lincoln's Leadership (Online)
Students will complete an online assessment based on the lesson objectives. The assessment will be scored by the computer. The attached answer key is the most current and may not coincide with previously printed guides.

TEACH
Activity 3. Optional: Lincoln's Leadership (Offline)
Instructions
In this optional activity, the student will memorize and recite the Gettysburg Address.

Learning Coach Guide
Lesson 9: The Brothers Grimm in Germany

In 1815, Germany was a group of many states and kingdoms bound together by a common language. But should the Germans be something more? The Brothers Grimm thought so. They collected German fairy tales and wrote a German dictionary, hoping to promote German nationalism.

Lesson Objectives

- Describe nineteenth-century Germany as a land made of many different kingdoms.
- Explain that the German language was the main common bond of these kingdoms.
- Recognize that the Brothers Grimm wanted to promote a sense of national identity and pride.
- Explain that the Brothers Grimm collected German folktales.

PREPARE

Approximate lesson time is 60 minutes.

Materials

For the Student

 Map of German Kingdoms, 1815

 History Journal

Keywords and Pronunciation

Albrecht Dürer (AHL-brekt DYOUR-ur)

folktale : A story or fairy tale that belongs to a certain land.

Frau Viehmann (frow FEE-mahn)

Jacob and Wilhelm Grimm (YAH-kub and VIL-helm grim)

Johannes Gutenberg (yoh-HAHN-uhs GOOT-n-burg)

TEACH
Activity 1: A Germany for Germans? (Online)
Instructions

The main teaching activity is online. Your student may complete this activity alone or with your help.

Activity 2: History Journal (Offline)
Instructions

With your student, read the History Journal entry for today's lesson and compare it with the sample paragraph below. Did it include the most important parts of the lesson?

You will use the History Journal to assess your student's understanding of this lesson.

The Brothers Grimm collected many folktales. They lived in the land we call Germany. At that time, Germany was divided into many kingdoms. The people there all spoke German, but they did not live in one country. The Brothers Grimm collected tales so people would remember them. They hoped the folktales would make Germans proud. The Brothers Grimm wanted Germans to think of themselves as one people.

Activity 3: Collecting Tales (Offline)
Instructions
Help your student collect titles of Brothers Grimm folktales.

Activity 4. Optional: The Brothers Grimm in Germany (Offline)
Instructions
In this optional activity, the student may either ask a parent or older relative to tell her one of their favorite fairy tales, or go to the library and find a Grimm's fairy tale that is new to her.

ASSESS
Lesson Assessment: The Brothers Grimm in Germany (Online)
Review your student's responses on the History journal activity, and input the results online. The attached answer key is the most current and may not coincide with previously printed guides.

Lesson Assessment Answer Key

The Brothers Grimm in Germany

Answers:

1. many different kingdoms
2. the German language
3. with a sense of national identity and pride
4. German folktales

Learning Coach Guide
Lesson 10: Bismarck Unites Germany

Before 1870, Germany was a confederation of several principalities and kingdoms. Otto von Bismarck forged them into a single nation. Bismarck was a statesman who believed that the great questions of the day would be settled by "blood and iron." He used a combination of shrewd strategy and military force to bring about his vision of a united Germany.

Lesson Objectives

- Recall that Germany was made up of many kingdoms.
- Describe Prussia as the most powerful German kingdom.
- Identify Otto von Bismarck as a Prussian statesman who united Germany into a single nation.
- Describe Bismarck as a man who believed in using "blood and iron" to settle tough problems.

PREPARE

Approximate lesson time is 60 minutes.

Materials

For the Student

⌨ Map of German Kingdoms, 1815-1871

History Journal

⌨ The Iron Chancellor Activity Sheet

Keywords and Pronunciation

chancellor : the title for the head of government in some countries

confederation : A group of states or kingdoms that are allied with each other.

Otto von Bismarck (AHT-oh fawn BIZ-mahrk)

prime minister : The title for the head of government in some countries.

TEACH
Activity 1: Man With a Mission *(Online)*

Instructions

This main teaching activity is online. Your student may want to complete this activity by herself, or you may want to join her at the computer as she reads how Bismark united Germany.

Activity 2: History Journal *(Offline)*

Instructions

With your student, read the History Journal entry for today's lesson and compare it with the sample paragraph below. Did it include the most important parts of the lesson?

Otto von Bismarck united Germany into one nation. Before Bismarck, Germany was made of many kingdoms. Bismarck was from Prussia. Prussia was the most powerful German kingdom. Bismarck had a plan to bring all the kingdoms together. He said he would do it using "blood and iron." Prussia went to war with France. The German kingdoms fought together to defeat France. Then they all became one nation.

Activity 3: The Iron Chancellor (Offline)
Instructions
Your student will complete the Iron Chancellor activity sheet to reinforce the lesson objectives.

ASSESS
Lesson Assessment: Bismark Unites Germany (Online)
Review your student's responses on The Iron Chancellor activity sheet, and input the results online. The attached answer key is the most current and may not coincide with previously printed guides.

Name _____   Date _____

Lesson Assessment Answer Key

Bismarck Unites Germany

Answers:

1. many

2. Prussia

3. Otto von Bismarck

4. blood and iron

5. Sample answer: Bismarck wanted to control the southern German states, but France stood in the way. He knew that if a war broke out between Prussia and France, the southern German states would have to choose sides and would choose to unite with Prussia.

Learning Coach Guide
Lesson 11: Garibaldi Fights for a United Italy

Once home to the Roman Empire and Renaissance greats, the peninsula was a collection of city-states that became united as the nation of Italy in the 1860s. Giuseppe Garibaldi was the military hero who helped liberate Italy and make it a united kingdom.

Lesson Objectives

- Explain that Italy was once divided into many city-states and kingdoms.
- Describe Giuseppe Garibaldi as a military leader who fought to unite Italy.
- Identify the Red Shirts as the name of Garibaldi's army.
- Explain that Italy became a single nation.

PREPARE

Approximate lesson time is 60 minutes.

Materials

For the Student

📖 Map of Italy, 1815-1870

History Journal

Keywords and Pronunciation

Alexandre Dumas (ahl-uhks-AHN-druh dyoo-MAH)
Cincinnatus (sin-sih-NAT-uhs)
Giuseppe Garibaldi (joo-ZEP-pay gah-ree-BAHL-dee)
Viva Garibaldi (VEE-vah gah-ree-BAHL-dee)

TEACH
Activity 1: The Making of Italy (Online)
Instructions

This teaching activity is online. Your student may want to complete this activity by herself, or you may want to join her at the computer as she reads about Garibaldi's efforts to unify Italy.

Activity 2: History Journal (Offline)
Instructions

With your student, read the History Journal entry for today's lesson and compare it with the sample paragraph below. Did it include the most important parts of the lesson?

Giuseppe Garibaldi led the fight to make Italy a united country. For a long time, Italy was divided into many kingdoms. Different princes and kings ruled them. Garibaldi helped the island of Sicily rebel. Then he led an army across Italy. His soldiers were called the Red Shirts. Garibaldi united Italy, but he did not become king. Instead, he went back to his home. He was happy that his country was finally united.

Activity 3: Wanted: A United Italy (Offline)
Instructions
Have your student design and create a recruiting poster for Garibaldi's Red Shirts.

ASSESS
Lesson Assessment: Bismarck Unites Germany (Online)
Students will complete an online assessment based on the lesson objectives. The assessment will be scored by the computer. The attached answer key is the most current and may not coincide with previously printed guides.

Learning Coach Guide
Lesson 12: The Olympics Revived

Nationalism and the growth of nation states affected recreation. For years people had dreamed of reviving the Olympic Games to give nations a way to compete not simply on the battlefield and in industry, but also in noble athletic competitions. The modern Olympic Games were born in 1896.

Lesson Objectives

- Recall that the modern Olympic Games had their origin in ancient Greece.
- Describe Baron de Coubertin as the father of the modern Olympic Games.
- State that the first modern Olympic Games were held in Athens.
- Describe the Olympics as international athletic competitions and a way for nations to compete peacefully.

PREPARE

Approximate lesson time is 60 minutes.

Keywords and Pronunciation

Demetrius Vikelas (duh-MEE-tree-uhs vee-KEH-luhs)

drachmas (DRAK-muhs)

Pierre de Coubertin (pyehr duh koo-behr-tan)

TEACH
Activity 1: The First Modern Olympics *(Online)*
Instructions

This teaching activity is online. Your student may want to complete this activity by herself, or you may want to join her at the computer as she reads about the revival of the Olympics.

Activity 2. Optional: Vikelas Writes Persuasively *(Offline)*
Instructions

Your student, as Demetrius Vikelas, will write a persuasive letter to convince the international community that the Olympics should be held in Greece.

ASSESS

Lesson Assessment: The Olympics Revived (*Online*)

Students will complete an online assessment based on the lesson objectives. The assessment will be scored by the computer. The attached answer key is the most current and may not coincide with previously printed guides.

TEACH
Activity 3. Optional: The Olympics Revived (Offline)
Instructions
Let your student and his friends compete in their own backyard Olympics.

Learning Coach Guide
Lesson 13: Unit Review and Assessment

The student will review this unit and take the unit assessment.

Lesson Objectives

- Demonstrate mastery of important knowledge and skills in this unit.
- Describe Peter the Great as a czar who tried to bring western ways to Russia.
- Explain that ideas about liberty, revolutions, and constitutions spread to Russia.
- Describe Nicholas as a czar whose reign was harsh, and who was dedicated to stopping the spread of those ideas.
- State that Nicholas was known as "the policeman of Europe."
- Explain that the southern states depended on plantation agriculture and slave labor.
- Explain that the northern states depended mainly on small farms, growing industry, and free labor.
- Describe the expansion of slavery into the new territories as the issue that divided North from South.
- Explain that after Abraham Lincoln was elected president, several southern states seceded from the Union.
- Describe the Civil War as the war that ended slavery and confirmed that the United States was a single nation.
- Identify Abraham Lincoln as president of the United States during the Civil War.
- Describe the Gettysburg Address as an important speech given by Lincoln during the Civil War.
- Describe nineteenth-century Germany as a land made of many different kingdoms.
- Explain that the German language was the main common bond of these kingdoms.
- Recognize that the Brothers Grimm wanted to promote a sense of national identity and pride.
- Describe Prussia as the most powerful German kingdom.
- Identify Otto von Bismarck as a Prussian statesman who united Germany into a single nation.
- Explain that Italy was once divided into many city-states and kingdoms.
- Describe Giuseppe Garibaldi as a military leader who fought to unite Italy.
- Explain that Italy became a single nation.
- Recall that the modern Olympic Games had their origin in ancient Greece.
- Describe the Olympics as international athletic competitions and a way for nations to compete peacefully.
- Explain that Catherine the Great expanded Russia to the Black Sea.
- Describe nationalism as a strong sense of pride in one's nation.
- Identify key figures and events that promoted nationalism (Ypsilanti, Lincoln, U.S. Civil War, Brothers Grimm, Bismarck, Garibaldi).
- Explain that the first modern Olympics began in the late 1800s with the growth of nationalism.

PREPARE

Approximate lesson time is 60 minutes.

TEACH
Activity 1: The Growth of Nations (Offline)
Instructions
The student will review this unit and take the unit assessment.

Answers:
[1] czars

[2] Peter the Great

[3] Catherine the Great

[4] the Black Sea

[5] serfs

[6] the Policeman of Europe

[7] the Ottoman Empire

[8] the Greeks

[9] They relied on slave labor.

[10] immigrants, small farmers, and city-folk

[11] Abraham Lincoln

[12] They seceded from the Union.

[13] The Gettysburg Address

[14] the Brothers Grimm

[15] Bismarck

[16] Garibaldi

[17] the Olympics

[18] in Athens, Greece

Activity 2: History Journal Review (Offline)
Instructions
The student will use the History Journal to review for the unit assessment. You can help by asking questions based on the work in the journal.

Activity 3: Online Interactive Review (Online)
Instructions
The student will continue reviewing the unit by completing an online, interactive review.

ASSESS

Unit Assessment: The Growth of Nations (Offline)
Students will complete an online assessment of the objectives covered so far in this unit. The assessment will be scored by the computer. The attached answer key is the most current and may not coincide with previously printed guides.

The Growth of Nations

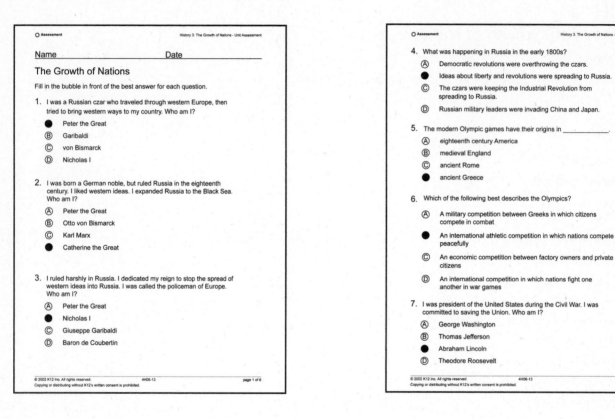

Name _____ Date _____

The Growth of Nations

Fill in the bubble in front of the best answer for each question.

1. I was a Russian czar who traveled through western Europe, then tried to bring western ways to my country. Who am I?
   - ● Peter the Great
   - Ⓑ Garibaldi
   - Ⓒ von Bismarck
   - Ⓓ Nicholas I

2. I was born a German noble, but ruled Russia in the eighteenth century. I liked western ideas. I expanded Russia to the Black Sea. Who am I?
   - Ⓐ Peter the Great
   - Ⓑ Otto von Bismarck
   - Ⓒ Karl Marx
   - ● Catherine the Great

3. I ruled harshly in Russia. I dedicated my reign to stop the spread of western ideas into Russia. I was called the policeman of Europe. Who am I?
   - Ⓐ Peter the Great
   - ● Nicholas I
   - Ⓒ Giuseppe Garibaldi
   - Ⓓ Baron de Coubertin

4. What was happening in Russia in the early 1800s?
   - Ⓐ Democratic revolutions were overthrowing the czars.
   - ● Ideas about liberty and revolutions were spreading to Russia.
   - Ⓒ The czars were keeping the Industrial Revolution from spreading to Russia.
   - Ⓓ Russian military leaders were invading China and Japan.

5. The modern Olympic games have their origins in _____.
   - Ⓐ eighteenth century America
   - Ⓑ medieval England
   - Ⓒ ancient Rome
   - ● ancient Greece

6. Which of the following best describes the Olympics?
   - Ⓐ A military competition between Greeks in which citizens compete in combat
   - ● An international athletic competition in which nations compete peacefully
   - Ⓒ An economic competition between factory owners and private citizens
   - Ⓓ An international competition in which nations fight one another in war games

7. I was president of the United States during the Civil War. I was committed to saving the Union. Who am I?
   - Ⓐ George Washington
   - Ⓑ Thomas Jefferson
   - ● Abraham Lincoln
   - Ⓓ Theodore Roosevelt

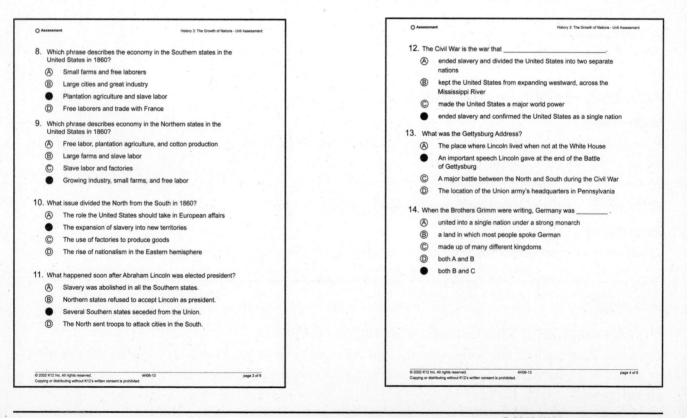

8. Which phrase describes the economy in the Southern states in the United States in 1860?
   - Ⓐ Small farms and free laborers
   - Ⓑ Large cities and great industry
   - ● Plantation agriculture and slave labor
   - Ⓓ Free laborers and trade with France

9. Which phrase describes economy in the Northern states in the United States in 1860?
   - Ⓐ Free labor, plantation agriculture, and cotton production
   - Ⓑ Large farms and slave labor
   - Ⓒ Slave labor and factories
   - ● Growing industry, small farms, and free labor

10. What issue divided the North from the South in 1860?
    - Ⓐ The role the United States should take in European affairs
    - ● The expansion of slavery into new territories
    - Ⓒ The use of factories to produce goods
    - Ⓓ The rise of nationalism in the Eastern hemisphere

11. What happened soon after Abraham Lincoln was elected president?
    - Ⓐ Slavery was abolished in all the Southern states.
    - Ⓑ Northern states refused to accept Lincoln as president.
    - ● Several Southern states seceded from the Union.
    - Ⓓ The North sent troops to attack cities in the South.

12. The Civil War is the war that _____.
    - Ⓐ ended slavery and divided the United States into two separate nations
    - Ⓑ kept the United States from expanding westward, across the Mississippi River
    - Ⓒ made the United States a major world power
    - ● ended slavery and confirmed the United States as a single nation

13. What was the Gettysburg Address?
    - Ⓐ The place where Lincoln lived when not at the White House
    - ● An important speech Lincoln gave at the end of the Battle of Gettysburg
    - Ⓒ A major battle between the North and South during the Civil War
    - Ⓓ The location of the Union army's headquarters in Pennsylvania

14. When the Brothers Grimm were writing, Germany was _____.
    - Ⓐ united into a single nation under a strong monarch
    - Ⓑ a land in which most people spoke German
    - Ⓒ made up of many different kingdoms
    - Ⓓ both A and B
    - ● both B and C

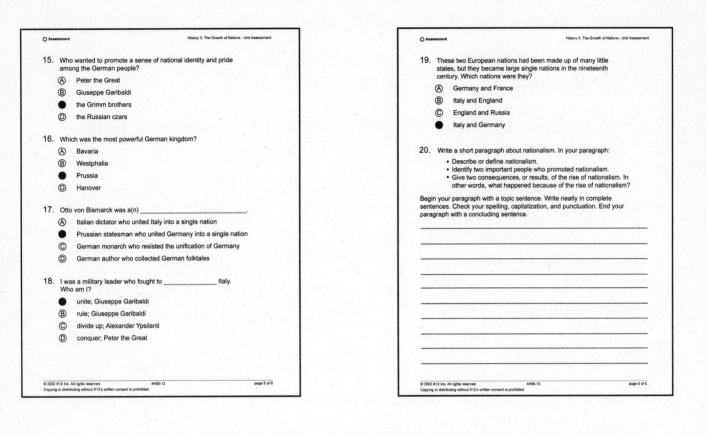

15. Who wanted to promote a sense of national identity and pride among the German people?

Ⓐ Peter the Great

Ⓑ Giuseppe Garibaldi

⬤ the Grimm brothers

Ⓓ the Russian czars

16. Which was the most powerful German kingdom?

Ⓐ Bavaria

Ⓑ Westphalia

⬤ Prussia

Ⓓ Hanover

17. Otto von Bismarck was a(n) _____.

Ⓐ Italian dictator who united Italy into a single nation

⬤ Prussian statesman who united Germany into a single nation

Ⓒ German monarch who resisted the unification of Germany

Ⓓ German author who collected German folktales

18. I was a military leader who fought to _____ Italy. Who am I?

⬤ unite; Giuseppe Garibaldi

Ⓑ rule; Giuseppe Garibaldi

Ⓒ divide up; Alexander Ypsilanti

Ⓓ conquer; Peter the Great

19. These two European nations had been made up of many little states, but they became large single nations in the nineteenth century. Which nations were they?

Ⓐ Germany and France

Ⓑ Italy and England

Ⓒ England and Russia

⬤ Italy and Germany

20. Write a short paragraph about nationalism. In your paragraph:

• Describe or define *nationalism*.
• Identify two important people who promoted nationalism.
• Give two consequences, or results, of the rise of nationalism. In other words, what happened because of the rise of nationalism?

Begin your paragraph with a topic sentence. Write neatly in complete sentences. Check your spelling, capitalization, and punctuation. End your paragraph with a concluding sentence.

_____

_____

_____

_____

_____

_____

_____

_____

_____

Scoring the Essay Question

This essay question is worth forty points. Score the student's writing as follows:

- Ten points for describing or defining nationalism as a strong sense of pride in one's nation.

- Ten points for identifying two people that promoted nationalism. The following are acceptable:

    o George Caleb Bingham
    o Abraham Lincoln
    o the Brothers Grimm
    o Otto von Bismarck
    o Alexander Ypsilanti
    o Giuseppe Garibaldi

- Ten points for each consequence or result of nationalism, for a maximum of twenty points. The following are acceptable:

    o The Olympics were revived.
    o Some new nations came into existence.
    o Many nations grew stronger.
    o Germany and Italy united into single countries.
    o Greece gained its independence from the Ottoman Empire.

Learning Coach Guide
Lesson 14: Semester Assessment

The student will take the semester assessment.

Lesson Objectives

- Demonstrate mastery of important knowledge and skills learned this semester.
- Demonstrate mastery of important knowledge and skills taught in previous lessons.
- Explain that Locke believed that if rulers governed badly, the people had a right of revolution.
- Identify Thomas Jefferson as the author of the Declaration of Independence.
- Identify the Constitutional Convention as the meeting in which the United States made a new plan of government.
- Describe Napoleon as the republican hero who became an all-powerful emperor.
- Explain that some colonists desired independence as they watched events in the young United States and in France.
- Explain that Bolívar led military campaigns to free much of Spanish America and is known as "the Liberator."
- Name capitalism as a system in which individuals and private companies make decisions about the economy.
- Explain that Marx predicted a revolution in which the working classes would rise up and overthrow the owners of industry.
- Recognize that the terms *Marxism* and *communism* refer to the work and theories of Karl Marx.
- Name Victoria as the British queen who reigned during this period.
- Describe Peter the Great as a czar who tried to bring western ways to Russia.
- Describe the Civil War as the war that ended slavery and confirmed that the United States was a single nation.
- Identify Abraham Lincoln as president of the United States during the Civil War.
- Recognize that the Brothers Grimm wanted to promote a sense of national identity and pride.
- Recall that Germany was made up of many kingdoms.
- Identify Otto von Bismarck as a Prussian statesman who united Germany into a single nation.
- Explain that Italy was once divided into many city-states and kingdoms.
- Name Great Britain's economy as the first capitalist economy.
- Recognize that Watt's steam engine could be used to power many machines.
- Name the American and French Revolutions as two great democratic revolutions.
- Describe a constitution as the basic law of government, which sets up the form of the government.
- Describe the Terror as a time of violence when many "enemies of the revolution" were killed.
- Explain that the French Revolution led to major European wars.
- Identify key figures, documents, and events in the American and French Revolutions (John Locke, Thomas Jefferson, James Madison, George Washington, Lafayette, Louis XVI, Robespierre, Napoleon, the Declaration of Independence, the U.S. Constitution, storming the Bastille, the Napoleonic Code, Waterloo).
- Explain that the Industrial Revolution began in England.

- Explain that during the Industrial Revolution production moved out of the home and into factories.
- Explain that in the early stages of the Industrial Revolution working conditions were harsh and workers suffered.
- Identify important figures, inventions, and ideas of the Industrial Revolution (James Watt, Robert Fulton, Charles Dickens, Karl Marx, spinning jenny, steam engine, steamboat, railroads, capitalism, Marxism).
- Describe the spread of democratic revolution to Latin America.
- Identify key figures and events of major revolutions in Latin America (including Toussaint L'Ouverture, Francisco Miranda, Miguel Hidalgo, Simon Bolívar).
- Describe the Scientific Revolution as a time of great progress in understanding nature.
- Explain that scientists used new methods of experimentation, obversation, and mathematics to understand nature.
- Identify key figures in the Scientific Revolution (Harvey, Hooke, Leeuwenhoek, Descartes, Newton, Franklin) and their contributions.
- Explain that people gained confidence in their ability to understand the laws of nature.

PREPARE

Approximate lesson time is 60 minutes.

TEACH
Activity 1: The Growth of Nations (Offline)
Instructions
Answers:
[1] the scientific method
[2] Thomas Jefferson
[3] in the Declaration of Independence
[4] the French Revolution
[5] Napoléon
[6] He was defeated.
[7] Karl Marx
[8] communism

Activity 2: End of Semester (Online)

ASSESS

Semester Assessment: History 4, Semester 1 (Offline)
Students will complete an offline Semester assessment. Print the assessment and have students complete it on their own. Use the answer key to score the assessment, and then enter the results online. The attached answer key is the most current and may not coincide with previously printed guides.

Semester Assessment

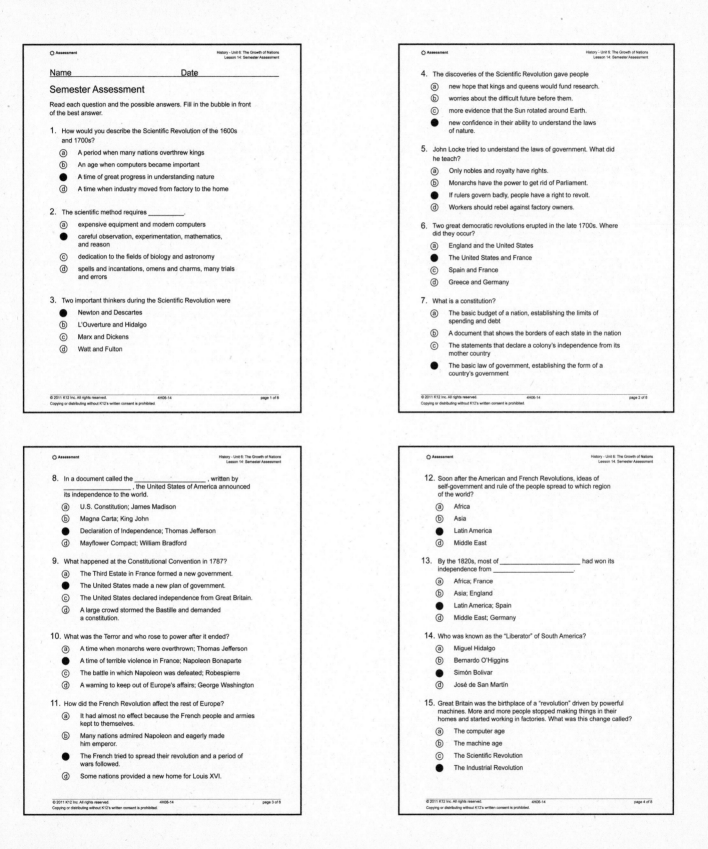

Name _____   Date _____

Semester Assessment

Read each question and the possible answers. Fill in the bubble in front of the best answer.

1. How would you describe the Scientific Revolution of the 1600s and 1700s?
   ⓐ A period when many nations overthrew kings
   ⓑ An age when computers became important
   ● A time of great progress in understanding nature
   ⓓ A time when industry moved from factory to the home

2. The scientific method requires _____.
   ⓐ expensive equipment and modern computers
   ● careful observation, experimentation, mathematics, and reason
   ⓒ dedication to the fields of biology and astronomy
   ⓓ spells and incantations, omens and charms, many trials and errors

3. Two important thinkers during the Scientific Revolution were
   ● Newton and Descartes
   ⓑ L'Ouverture and Hidalgo
   ⓒ Marx and Dickens
   ⓓ Watt and Fulton

4. The discoveries of the Scientific Revolution gave people
   ⓐ new hope that kings and queens would fund research.
   ⓑ worries about the difficult future before them.
   ⓒ more evidence that the Sun rotated around Earth.
   ● new confidence in their ability to understand the laws of nature.

5. John Locke tried to understand the laws of government. What did he teach?
   ⓐ Only nobles and royalty have rights.
   ⓑ Monarchs have the power to get rid of Parliament.
   ● If rulers govern badly, people have a right to revolt.
   ⓓ Workers should rebel against factory owners.

6. Two great democratic revolutions erupted in the late 1700s. Where did they occur?
   ⓐ England and the United States
   ● The United States and France
   ⓒ Spain and France
   ⓓ Greece and Germany

7. What is a constitution?
   ⓐ The basic budget of a nation, establishing the limits of spending and debt
   ⓑ A document that shows the borders of each state in the nation
   ⓒ The statements that declare a colony's independence from its mother country
   ● The basic law of government, establishing the form of a country's government

8. In a document called the _____, written by _____, the United States of America announced its independence to the world.
   ⓐ U.S. Constitution; James Madison
   ⓑ Magna Carta; King John
   ● Declaration of Independence; Thomas Jefferson
   ⓓ Mayflower Compact; William Bradford

9. What happened at the Constitutional Convention in 1787?
   ⓐ The Third Estate in France formed a new government.
   ● The United States made a new plan of government.
   ⓒ The United States declared independence from Great Britain.
   ⓓ A large crowd stormed the Bastille and demanded a constitution.

10. What was the Terror and who rose to power after it ended?
   ⓐ A time when monarchs were overthrown; Thomas Jefferson
   ● A time of terrible violence in France; Napoleon Bonaparte
   ⓒ The battle in which Napoleon was defeated; Robespierre
   ⓓ A warning to keep out of Europe's affairs; George Washington

11. How did the French Revolution affect the rest of Europe?
   ⓐ It had almost no effect because the French people and armies kept to themselves.
   ⓑ Many nations admired Napoleon and eagerly made him emperor.
   ● The French tried to spread their revolution and a period of wars followed.
   ⓓ Some nations provided a new home for Louis XVI.

12. Soon after the American and French Revolutions, ideas of self-government and rule of the people spread to which region of the world?
   ⓐ Africa
   ⓑ Asia
   ● Latin America
   ⓓ Middle East

13. By the 1820s, most of _____ had won its independence from _____.
   ⓐ Africa; France
   ⓑ Asia; England
   ● Latin America; Spain
   ⓓ Middle East; Germany

14. Who was known as the "Liberator" of South America?
   ⓐ Miguel Hidalgo
   ⓑ Bernardo O'Higgins
   ● Simón Bolívar
   ⓓ José de San Martín

15. Great Britain was the birthplace of a "revolution" driven by powerful machines. More and more people stopped making things in their homes and started working in factories. What was this change called?
   ⓐ The computer age
   ⓑ The machine age
   ⓒ The Scientific Revolution
   ● The Industrial Revolution

Semester Assessment

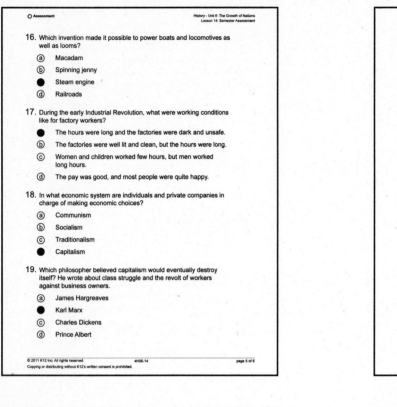

16. Which invention made it possible to power boats and locomotives as well as looms?

   (a) Macadam

   (b) Spinning jenny

   ● **Steam engine**

   (d) Railroads

17. During the early Industrial Revolution, what were working conditions like for factory workers?

   ● **The hours were long and the factories were dark and unsafe.**

   (b) The factories were well lit and clean, but the hours were long.

   (c) Women and children worked few hours, but men worked long hours.

   (d) The pay was good, and most people were quite happy.

18. In what economic system are individuals and private companies in charge of making economic choices?

   (a) Communism

   (b) Socialism

   (c) Traditionalism

   ● **Capitalism**

19. Which philosopher believed capitalism would eventually destroy itself? He wrote about class struggle and the revolt of workers against business owners.

   (a) James Hargreaves

   ● **Karl Marx**

   (c) Charles Dickens

   (d) Prince Albert

20. Which very productive country had the world's first capitalist economy?

   (a) France

   (b) Portugal

   (c) Germany

   ● **Great Britain**

21. Karl Marx's idea that property and wealth should be held in common by all the people is called _____.

   ● **communism**

   (b) traditionalism

   (c) capitalism

   (d) federalism

22. Who ruled England at the height of the Industrial Revolution?

   (a) Prince Albert

   (b) King George III

   ● **Queen Victoria**

   (d) Catherine the Great

23. He was so excited about the Scientific and Industrial Revolutions in the west that he tried to bring western ways to Russia. Who was he?

   ● **Peter the Great**

   (b) Nicholas II

   (c) Prince Albert

   (d) Karl Marx

24. Bismarck united many small states into this single nation. And the Brothers Grimm collected fairy tales to help give the people a sense of national identity. What place was this?

   ● **Germany**

   (b) France

   (c) Italy

   (d) Russia

25. Which two European nations had been many little states until they became large single nations in the nineteenth century?

   (a) Italy and England

   (b) England and Russia

   ● **Italy and Germany**

   (d) Germany and France

26. Who was the U.S. president during the Civil War?

   (a) George Washington

   (b) Thomas Jefferson

   ● **Abraham Lincoln**

   (d) Theodore Roosevelt

27. The Civil War is the war that _____.

   ● **ended slavery and confirmed the United States as a single nation**

   (b) ended slavery and divided the United States into two separate nations

   (c) kept the United States from expanding westward, across the Mississippi River

   (d) made the United States a major world power

Match each revolution on the left with the people on the right who played important roles in the revolution.

28. **B** Scientific   A. James Watt, Robert Fulton

    C Democratic   B. William Harvey, Isaac Newton

    A Industrial   C. Thomas Jefferson, Simon Bolivar